FOSTERING HOPE

Smyth & Helwys Publishing, Inc.
6316 Peake Road
Macon, Georgia 31210-3960
1-800-747-3016
©2022 by Robert W. Lee
All rights reserved.

Author photo courtesy of
Katelyn Alexandria Photography

Fostering Hope Catawba Valley is a nonprofit organization dedicated to helping foster children in their region through service and support. They graciously agreed to allow us to use their name for our book title. Please consider making a donation at www.fosteringhopecatawba.com/donate.

Library of Congress Cataloging-in-Publication Data

Names: Lee, Rob, 1992- editor.
Title: Fostering hope : a prayer book for foster and adoptive families /
edited by Robert W. Lee.
Description: Macon, GA : Smyth & Helwys Publishing, [2022]
Identifiers: LCCN 2022023304 | ISBN 9781641733847 (paperback)
Subjects: LCSH: Parents--Prayers and devotions. | Adoption--Religious
aspects--Christianity. | Foster parents--Prayers and devotions. |
Adoptive parents--Prayers and devotions. | Children--Prayers and
devotions.
Classification: LCC BV4529 .F67 2022 | DDC 248.8/45--dc23/eng/20220711
LC record available at https://lccn.loc.gov/2022023304

FOSTERING HOPE

*A Prayer Book for
Foster and Adoptive Families*

EDITED BY ROBERT W. LEE
Foreword by Chanequa Walker-Barnes

Also by Robert W. Lee

Stained-Glass Millennials

A Sin by Any Other Name
Reckoning with Racism and the Heritage of the South

The Pulpit and the Paper
A Pastor's Coming of Age in Newsprint

Advance Praise for *Fostering Hope*

This is a beautiful new spiritual resource for all the beautiful new families that, with each passing day, bless our world more and more.

—James Martin, SJ
Author of *Learning to Pray*

What a powerful collection of prayers! As I read through them and let them echo in my soul, my heart was moved and expanded. A gift for families of all types, including yours.

—Brian D. McLaren
Author of *Do I Stay Christian?*

This is a beautiful volume of prayers and reflections—one that captures much of the nuance and complexity of adoption and seeks to give voice to the variety of people at the center of adoption stories. The book gives space for raw grief and for glimmers of grace, without being overly saccharine about the adoption journey. With its prayers of lament, gratitude, joy, and frustration, this slim volume pricks the heart and stands to encourage any whose lives are touched by adoption and fostering.

—The Rev. Meghan F. Benson
Chaplain, Duke Divinity School

Simply put, this book of prayers, edited by Robert W. Lee, one of the bright lights in of our world, is inspired. It is chock-full of collective wisdom and comfort, wonder and challenge, power and strength, and joy and sorrow. Had it been around when my sons were growing up, it would have had a prominent spot on my night stand next to my Bible and Book of Common Prayer. By now its pages would be worn and dog-eared from use. If you are the parent of a child

—foster, adopted, or biological—*Fostering Hope: A Prayerbook for Foster and Adoptive Families* is for you.

—The Very Rev. Samuel Colley-Toothaker
Dean, St. James Cathedral, Fresno, California

Having recently become an adoptive grandparent, reading through these pages touched deep places in our experience and prepared me for things that lie ahead. The prayers resonate with thoughtful spiritual insight, bold honesty, and deep love. Along with providing a devotional resource, it made me aware of things I had not considered and will be a beautiful gift of wisdom, guidance, and faith to everyone who shares in the experience of adoption.

—The Rev. Dr. James A. Harnish
Retired United Methodist pastor
Author of *Finding Your Bearings: How Words that Guided Jesus through Crisis Can Guide Us*

For Phoenix and Athena
I pray for you every day.
You and your mom are my everything.

Acknowledgments

A work like this takes time and effort. This is my first time editing a complete prayer book, and it was like herding the best group of cats imaginable. To everyone who contributed, I am grateful and humbled by your presence in this book, even if it felt like pulling teeth sometimes. To my family—Phoenix, Athena, and Stephanie—I am forever in your debt for being willing to put up with my authorial and editorial tendencies while writing. To my children's grandparents, Nona and Crabby (Sherrie and Rusty) and Gigi and Pepe (Kathy and Keith), I continue to be grateful for your witness and example. To their great-grandparents, Barbara and Bob Lee, Carol and Mickey Robinette, and Sam Sansoucy, I am grateful we have your continued guidance in our lives.

To my dear cousin Samantha Hodges and colleague Mindy Grassel, thanks for being my travel buddies and sounding boards as this book was birthed—I cannot thank you enough for your presence in my life. To the Rev. Mandy McDow, thank you for always being a friend in this process; that, along with being Athena's godmother, is the best combination ever. To the Rev. Nathan Kirkpatrick, you remain a guide in all things life and liturgy, and your being a part of our extended family as a godparent means so much.

To the essayists, Kimberly, Josh, and Kate, it was a joy to walk with you and have to do so little to see your light shining through your words. The joy of being an editor is when you have to do very little, and you all gave me that gift.

To Katelyn Byng, who helped with my headshot, I consider your friendship and your talents an amazing gift to me and to the world. To my publisher, Smyth & Helwys; publisher Keith Gammons; and editor Leslie Andres, your patience, kindness, and advice have not been lost on me. I am so grateful this book came to pass.

A note on the book's title: Fostering Hope Catawba Valley is a nonprofit organization dedicated to helping foster children in the region through service and support. They graciously agreed to allow us to use their name for the title. Please consider making a donation to Fostering Hope at www.fosteringhopecatawba. com/donate.

Contents

Part 3: On Endings

"Unrevealed until its season, something God alone can see."
—Natalie Sleeth, "Hymn of Promise"

Contributors

Some names are shortened or altered by request of the individual.
Every effort was made to respect their privacy.

Sue B. is an author, business consultant, coach, and interfaith chaplain. An adoptive mother of two, she considers parenthood the most profound love journey of life.

Jay Bakker is a pastor and the son of famous televangelists. He works toward understanding grace and hope in spite of one's history.

The Rev. Heidi Bolt is a licensed foster parent and ordained minister. She currently serves as co-pastor with her husband in Red Wing, Minnesota, where they live with their two children.

The Rev. Lauren Boyd is a United Methodist pastor in Denver, Colorado.

Frankie Boyko is a nonprofit professional living in Chicago, Illinois. She cherishes the relationships she has with adopted members of her family.

Kimberly L. Carter, MBA, MDiv is a Millennial Women's Leadership Trainer who specializes in women's empowerment training, coaching, and speaking. Kimberly is currently a doctoral student at the California Institute of Integral Studies (CIIS) in the Women's Spirituality PhD department and a fellow with the Center for Writing and Scholarship.

The Rev. Cindy Cushman is an ordained minister in the Presbyterian Church (USA). She and her husband adopted four children from foster care.

The Rev. Dr. Charles "Charlie" Dupree is Rector at St. Paul's Episcopal Church in Richmond, Virginia.

The Rev. Lisa Fischbeck is the recently retired founding vicar of the Church of the Advocate in Chapel Hill, North Carolina, and the stepmother of an adopted child.

The Rev. Elizabeth Hagan is a pastor, author, and adoptive mama making her home these days in Athens, Georgia. She wrote about her and her husband's journey to parenthood in the book *Birthed: Finding Grace through Infertility*.

The Rev. Dr. Erin Robinson Hall writes and ministers from her home in Macon, Georgia. She can be found at erinrobinsonhall.com or chasing her four kids, both biological and adopted, around any playground they can find.

The Rev. Paige Alvarez Hanks is an Episcopal priest blessed with two amazing humans who joined the family through foster care and a sister who heroically gave her family the opportunity to love them unconditionally.

The Rev. Will Hasley is a United Methodist pastor and adoptive parent living in Charlottesville, Virginia.

The Rev. Sarah Heath is a pastor, creator, and podcaster who lives in Costa Mesa, California.

The Rev. Joey Heath-Mason is an adoptive parent and United Methodist pastor in the Washington, D.C., area.

The Rev. Amanda Hines is an adoptive mother of three brave, beautiful, and resilient children. She is an ordained minister in the Presbyterian Church (USA) who has served congregations in the PC (USA) and the Christian Church (Disciples of Christ) in Indiana, Kentucky, North Carolina, and Virginia. She is also a trained mindfulness teacher with a special interest in contemplative prayer and mindfulness.

Katie Hines (age 13) wants other adopted children to know the unconditional love of God and the hope she finds through faith.

William Hines (age 10) wants other adopted children to know that prayer can help you.

Xavier Hines (age 11) wants other adopted children to know that God loves you no matter what.

The Rev. Dr. James C. Howell is the senior minister at Myers Park United Methodist Church in Charlotte, North Carolina.

Marissa Joyce is a dreamer, a reader, an over-committer, and a creator. She is married to an amazingly patient man and is also a mother (adoptive and otherwise) to three small humans. She lives in Winston-Salem, North Carolina, in a house full of toys, art supplies, and dog fur. Over the past three years, God has completely turned her world upside down in a messy but beautiful way.

Laura Knobel works in alumni relations and serves as a church leader in Minnesota, where she lives with her husband, Nate, and their two sons, both adopted from foster care.

Jennifer Lawrence is the daughter of a foster child, mom to Elle and Jake, grandma to three grandchildren, and a third-generation vestment maker living on the Redlands Coast, Queensland, Australia.

Athena Lee (age 4) is the adopted daughter of Robert and Stephanie Lee. She loves singing and princesses.

The Rev. Robert W. Lee is the editor of this book and the author of three other books. An ordained minister, he lives in Statesville, North Carolina, with his wife and two adopted children.

Stephanie Lee is an adoptive parent to two girls and a marketing professional in North Carolina.

The Rt. Rev. Frank Logue is diocesan bishop for the Diocese of Georgia.

The Rev. Mandy McDow is the mother of three and godmother to an adopted child. She serves as senior minister at First United Methodist Church in Los Angeles, California.

The Rev. Leo Morton is an adoptive parent and senior pastor of Unifour Church in Newton, North Carolina.

The Rev. Dr. Jerusha Neal is associate professor of homiletics at Duke University Divinity School in Durham, North Carolina.

The Rev. Joshua Olds (DMin candidate, Columbia International University) is a public theologian and pastor of A Place for the Wanderer, an online community for those who feel displaced or discouraged by the church. He also serves as executive editor of lifeisstory.com and hosts the *Beyond the Page* podcast. Josh is currently an American expat living in the United Kingdom, learning from the Anglican tradition, and serving wherever God places him.

Kelsie Olds is a pediatric occupational therapist and mom of two. She can be found waxing poetic about everything from disability and inclusion to dinosaurs and duct tape at The Occuplaytional Therapist (@occuplaytional) on social media.

The Rev. Brandon Patterson is an adoptive/foster parent and senior pastor of Amelia Christian Church in Clayton, North Carolina.

The Rev. Peter Preble is an ordained minister serving at a United Methodist Church in Hull, Massachusetts.

Kate Rademacher is an author, foster parent, and professional in international public health living in Chapel Hill, North Carolina, with her family. She is the author of three books, including *Their Faces Shone: A Foster Parent's Lessons on Loving and Letting Go*, a memoir about her experience as a foster parent. A graduate of Wesleyan University in Connecticut and the University of North Carolina at Chapel Hill, Kate's professional work is focused on international public health. Her other two books, *Following the Red Bird: First Steps into a Life of Faith* and *Reclaiming Rest: The Promise of Sabbath, Solitude, and Stillness in a Restless World*, explore themes of faith, discernment, and how we can rest in God even as we navigate the challenges of daily life.

Valerie and Michelle Rogers are foster and adoptive parents and the co-founders of Anchor Hope, a nonprofit that supports children coming into foster care. They are members of Christ UMC in Greensboro, North Carolina, where they attend with their adopted son and foster daughter.

The Rev. Rob Rollins is a retired United Methodist minister.

Kathleen Sansoucy is the grandmother of two adoptive grandchildren. Affectionately known as Gigi, she lives in Wake Forest, North Carolina.

The Rev. Dr. H. Stephen Shoemaker is pastor of Grace Baptist Church in Statesville, North Carolina.

Rabbi Michael Siegel is senior rabbi at Anshe Emet Synagogue in Chicago, Illinois.

The Rev. Dr. Chris Thomas is pastor of the First Baptist Church of Wilson, North Carolina, where he lives with his wife, Sallie, and their two adopted children, Kohl and Carter.

The Rev. Dr. Chanequa Walker-Barnes is professor of practical theology and pastoral counseling at Columbia Theological Seminary. An accomplished author and pastor, she is also an adoptive parent.

Foreword

Chanequa Walker-Barnes, PhD

When my husband and I became parents via adoption, a relative casually mentioned to me, "I'm jealous. You got to skip being pregnant. You did it the easy way."

Nothing about fostering and adopting is easy, not for the foster and adoptive parents, the child, or the birth parents. A foster or adoption situation almost always means that something has not gone according to plan. Maybe a person or couple has become pregnant when they do not want to be. Perhaps a person who wants to parent has been unable to do so, hindered by poverty, trauma, mental illness, addiction, and so on. A child may have been removed from their biological family by the child welfare system. Perhaps the adoptive or foster parents have suffered through fertility problems, miscarriage, or the loss of biological children.

Even the smoothest adoption processes happen on an unpredictable timetable. For some parents-in-waiting, it involves years filled with one heartbreak after another: being unmatched, failed matches, having to relinquish foster children for whom they hoped to provide a forever family. When the transition to parenthood happens, it is often sudden. One day you're not a parent, and then you get a call and suddenly you are. There is no time to prepare, no time to nest, no time to plan for time off work. Suddenly, in the midst of all your other roles and responsibilities, you're a new parent. There is nothing easy about that, whether you've waited for mere weeks or several years.

We became parents through private adoption. Our son's birth mother chose us—a couple whom she had never met—to raise him. We brought him home when he was ten days old. From the beginning, he has been "our own." I could not imagine loving anyone more. He is so like me and my husband that sometimes I've wondered, "Did I birth this boy?" I grieve that it was not my womb that carried him. So does he. It feels like we were meant to be together. Our "happily ever after" has some painful undersides. Somewhere out there is a woman only known to us as "Michelle," who may at times deeply grieve her decision not to parent, even though she believed she was doing the right thing. There are unknown biological family stories and histories that are part of who my son is. There are repeated moments when we encounter adoption stigma that creeps up in how children's movies represent adoption or that sends your kid home crying because an elementary school classmate teased him mercilessly upon finding out that he was adopted.

There is no easy path to, through, or beyond forming families through fostering and adoption, which take the normal challenges of parenting and raise them a few degrees. The contributors of this book have written honestly and transparently to God about the many complex feelings and experiences of adoption and fostering. They have overcome the shame and secrecy of adoption stigma to express publicly the longings and anxieties of parents and children.

There are prayers here for the unique needs of foster and adoptive families: peace and patience during the waiting; the longing to be chosen; wisdom and support for the social workers and other professionals who hold the fates of families in their hands; smooth transition after placement; cross-racial and international adoption issues; mental health issues; the needs of birth parents and siblings; aging out of foster care systems; navigating questions about the past or about family histories; adoptees re-navigating any wounds regarding their adoption at different developmental periods; saying goodbye to a foster child.

But the lives of foster and adoption families do not just revolve around how the family was formed. We experience the same developmental traditions and growing-up experiences as biologically intact families. Thus, I am especially grateful for the "ordinary" prayers in this book: prayers about baptism, graduation, weddings, and death; marriage, divorce, and blended families; gender, sexuality, and racial identity development; even frustration during the teenage years.

May God—and the world—hear our prayers.

Introduction

As I began this prayerbook project in the fall of 2021, I was already working on a devotional for a local congregation for Christmas. Indeed, clergy often work far in advance and then fly by the seat of their pants, and this project is no different. The assigned text for the devotional is all too familiar to me after attending seminary and preparing for the holidays from John's Gospel, but this year it took on new and abundant life: "And the Word became flesh and lived among us, and we have seen his glory, the glory as of a father's only son" (John 1:14). This past year, my wife and I adopted two amazing, precocious, precious girls. They are currently ages three and four, full of life and love and compassion after their young lives have already seen such pain. They are my heart outside of my body and my new means of experiencing what it means to be a father loving a child and wanting the world to know that child for who they are.

I can attest that Phoenix and Athena Lee are far from being Jesus of Nazareth, especially when it's time for them to share with each other. But the incarnation of love that a parent has for a child takes on new life for me this year, this season, this existence. I have come to know Scripture in all its beauty better because of my interactions here and now. The liveliness of Scripture allows us to see ourselves in the stories and the stories in ourselves.

This book is both an incomplete and complete attempt to see ourselves in a story. Maybe you've picked it up for yourself and found it to be a good start. Perhaps you're picking it up for a family and the new, overwhelming journey they are taking—either way, I welcome you to the world of fostering and adoption. My understanding is that prayer books invite us into a story; they are not the completeness or wholeness of the story but the catalyst by which we enter it, the gateway by which we mark our entry into a new and different way of experiencing the fullness of a life-giving and loving God.

This prayer book does not have all the answers for all scenarios, but it does offer a wellspring of experience from those who know fostering or adoptions well and from those who have walked alongside others in these journeys. Those who have written prayers for this short book include clergy and laypeople; men, women, and non-binary folk; gay and straight; Black and white; well-off and struggling. They encompass, as you will see, the beauty of what God is doing in the peculiar world of adoption and foster care.

I hope this book will bring you joy, cause you to pause, and ultimately take you deeper into your own story. I hope it beckons you to find yourself and others in the Divine dance that has been calling you toward itself since before you could remember. I hope it engages and directs you toward your Creator. Most of all, I hope you find the love expressed in these pages to be compelling and pointing toward God, in whom we find our hope and our salvation. I'm grateful to experience my adopted girls in my life, and now I have a book to guide me in prayer for and with them all the days of my life.

How to Use This Book

My hope in putting together a book like this is not that it would be a tool for conversion or proselytization of children in anyone's care. Plenty of books attempt this maneuver, and they are dangerous. They not only raise the specter of Christian colonialization but also suggest that they have answers when they emphatically do not. Instead, this book suggests that the questions surrounding foster and adoptive care are bigger than any earthly answer we might be able to muster. That is where we find God both for us and with us.

For us and with us. Sam Wells, vicar of St. Martin's in the Fields in London and former dean of Duke Chapel, suggests that both "for" and "with" suggest different parts of the economy of God's presence with humankind. It is my hope that this prayer book can dial into the same economy. I hope you see the blessed *with-ness* of collaboration and connection that these prayers offer while also knowing that we are all rooting, praying, and yearning with you. Romans 8:26 comes to mind: "Likewise the Spirit helps us in our weakness; for we do not know how to pray as we ought, but that very Spirit intercedes with sighs too deep for words." In the orbit of foster care and adoption, these contributors and I have felt that Spirit interceding on our behalf. We have all found ourselves not knowing quite how to encapsulate a prayer, a thought, an idea to God in this process. I hope this book reassures you that you are not alone. You are a precious child of God, just like the child now in your care.

The *for-ness* of God is that God advocates on our behalf, and the *with-ness* suggests an abiding and steadfast presence through the years. This book provides both realities in a simple concept. Your situation may be unique, but in God's holy wisdom God gave us a way to be unique while also making connections: through solidarity with others who are going through a similar experience. The prayers in this book may not all fit perfectly with your unique scenario and perspective, but I guarantee that the people who wrote them stand in solidarity with you. Their prayers provide a balm for the weary soul that has been up too late with the children only to rise early to make sure they get to school on time.

A Confession on Prayer

As a clergyperson who grew up in the Methodist tradition, I am well versed in the fact that prayer's identity is found in confession, thanksgiving, and petition. In that spirit, I will first confess that there are times when my prayer life is less than ideal. Some of us might be given the gift of prayer and supplication, but some of us have to work at it a little more than others.

As someone who has to work at it, prayer books have always guided me. They are tried and true methods in some ways, but they also offer fresh expressions of grace each time the prayers are offered. You might need to edit or slightly adjust some of the prayers in this book, and everyone who wrote these prayers blessed and encouraged that when necessary. Prayer, both personal and corporate, is founded on the need to be in communion with God. Our main goal in creating this book is to encourage that communion.

If the next part of prayer is thanksgiving, then I must give context for the dedication of this book. In 2020, I was pastoring a church in Newton, North Carolina, that had a robust foster care ministry. Two of my dearest church members, Erin and LaDarla Lioret, had two girls in foster care at their home whose plan changed, and the children were being relinquished to the adoption process. My wife, Stephanie, was teaching Sunday school, and when she heard, she ran to me and exclaimed, "What do you think?" The rest has been one deep breath. Both of us knew that Stephanie's intuition was right—these girls were meant for us out of circumstances beyond their control. I recognize this wasn't the ideal scenario—we were told in our classes with the Department of Social Services that reunification with a biological family is always the ultimate goal—but in a greater sense, this is how our family's story was always supposed to unfold.

We enlisted as foster parent wannabes, taking classes, being interviewed, and sitting on pins and needles every time the phone rang. It was odd because, though we knew the girls we wanted to adopt, we had to be treated as if that wasn't the case—that we had no insider knowledge and could receive any placement Social Services might choose. At times, Stephanie and I wondered why we had committed ourselves to such a broken and fragile institution, only to be quickly reminded why each Sunday when we saw the girls. During this painstaking process, we were required not to let the girls discover our desired plans, and I had the complicated role of pastoring the children I wanted to parent. To them, I was Pastor Rob for a short season of their lives. And then God's handiwork fell into place. In the holy wisdom meant for fairy tales, the girls' biological parents elected to sign over their children to us as a means of getting them to a place of safety, security, and peace. This action on their part deserves gratitude and praise, despite former misgivings. The girls have a home now, a place where they will grow and flourish and come to know all the things that matter most.

On Valentine's Day weekend of 2021, Athena and Phoenix came to live with us. In July of that year the adoption was finalized and complete in the eyes of the state—though it had happened much sooner in our hearts.

Finally, this book is steeped in petition. As a parent, I have found myself praying more fervently. I am more concerned with the future and with living long enough to see it through to fruition. The picture is much bigger now and in greater color than ever before. This book invites you to pray without ceasing and to experience God with you. The roots of our faith are built in community and communication, and through our petitions we communicate to God the needs of those we love most and the needs of the community and world in which we all live. This standard of prayer is the basis for a life in communion with God. May we be bold in approaching the throne of grace with our confessions, our thanksgiving, and our petitions.

We're All Together Now

I love how Ram Dass describes connecting with others: "We're all just walking each other home" (*How Can I Help?* [New York: Knopf, 1985], 236). I was baptized on All Saints' Day 1992 at Broad Street United Methodist Church in Statesville, North Carolina. On May 27, 2021, our girls were baptized into the faith at the same font at the same church—by their dad, no less. We're all on this journey together, and we're working through the journey as each day passes. We grow in grace and compassion for each other, and we find God there. Perhaps the gift of fostering and adoption is that we have to learn at a quicker and more adept speed than we do in other situations, and we have no handbook to guide us. But we do have a prayer book now. We have a way of getting past the sleepless nights and the long days. We have the potential to reach out and reach in through this family journey. God is never done with our stories, as I never expected my journey to include two beautiful, precocious, kind, and bright-eyed girls from another family of origin.

In this book, may you experience the story that is still being written. May you find yourself and each other in this book, and may God hear your prayers and supplications. May you hear the clarion call to care for the orphan and the adoptee and the foster child. May you accept that call in the fullness of time for the sake of your salvation and the salvation of the world. Thanks be to God. Amen.

—*The Rev. Robert W. Lee*
Statesville, North Carolina
Summer 2022

Part 1

On Beginnings

The Rev. Joshua Olds

"In my end is my beginning." —T. S. Eliot, *Four Quartets*

Life Interrupted

It was an afternoon in June when we got the phone call.

It had already been a stressful week. Just the day before, I'd pulled aside church leadership for a meeting to let them know that I'd be stepping down as associate pastor. My wife, Kelsie, and I were finally moving forward with our plans to travel the country. In the past eighteen months, she had graduated and moved into her career. We had completed the adoption of a beautiful baby boy. As a family of three, we were ready to move on to the next stage of life, starting a new adventure to see what God had in store for us.

We had it all planned out. Her field allowed her to take three-month contracts working in various cities. We would stay in short-term lodgings, visit friends from coast to coast, and see what ministry opportunities fell our way. I planned to pursue a doctorate and take a much-needed sabbatical after several years of full-time pastoring tacked onto a full-time job as a gymnastics coach. Once we felt settled in a place, we would stay there and start our new life.

And then the phone call came. I was at my coaching job when someone from the front office came to get me. "Kelsie's here and she needs to talk to you now." As we sat in my car in the parking lot, she laid it all out: Our son's first mother was pregnant. She called the adoption agency. The adoption agency called us. *Would we want to adopt the baby?*

This was completely unexpected. We had spent years saving up to pay for the last adoption and were just now recovering from those expenses. We had made these plans to move for years and had just begun to put them into action— including telling our church family that we were leaving. Just a couple hours before the phone call that changed everything, I was in the owner's office at the gymnastics center telling them they needed to find a new coach. This was a major disruption to our plans. It meant undoing so much of what we had envisioned for our lives.

But there wasn't a moment of hesitation. *Yes, we'll do it.* In ten minutes, we undid the secret plans we'd had ever since our son's adoption finalized. I went back inside, recanted my two-week notice, and started planning for the future. We had six months before welcoming baby number two to the family.

It is impossible to plan for adoption. Every single case is unique and has its own timeline. I'm convinced that there's no such thing as a typical adoption journey. We all just get thrust into the messiness and have to trust God to work it out. It's impossible to plan in any major way because you're literally not in control. It's an exercise in faith. For my son, we signed the paperwork six months before matching with him, and then he was born the day we were chosen as his parents. With this adoption, we went from not planning to adopt another child—and even actively pursuing things that would prevent us from adopting—to having a six-month countdown to prepare for the baby's arrival.

God's Will?

In the following months, more than one person asked me how we could make a decision like that—completely alter our lives in unchangeable ways in the span of ten minutes. *How do you know this is God's will?* That's a very good question. In the ten minutes my wife and I discussed whether to adopt this baby, the question of God's will never came up. It's not that we didn't consider it; it's that we already knew that God had called us to care for this family through adoption, that God wants children to have loving parents, and that God wants families to be together. God's will was obvious: babies need families. How do you say no to a baby in need of a family just because their existence doesn't fit your ideal plans?

God's will was obvious. The question was whether or not we wanted to be a part of it. At great personal cost, we chose to follow where it seemed God was leading. We didn't need to pray for a certain length of time or throw out a fleece like Gideon. We knew God's will and simply had to decide whether or not we would be faithful to it. We chose to go on the journey and let God refine and redirect along the way.

Too often, people seeking the will of God never do anything because they're always waiting on more evidence that God is calling them. You may be on that fence right now, wondering if God is calling you to adoption or foster care. I can't speak to your exact circumstances, but I know this: God loves children and wants them to be in good families. Start the journey and let God define and refine it. But be aware; the journey gets messy.

Six months passed and we didn't adopt that baby. There's a lot to the story, but very little of it is something that I can share because it's not mine to tell. My wife and I were broken. Utterly devastated. We had altered everything in our lives and then . . . nothing. Not only did we not have a baby, but we didn't even have the life we imagined. We'd spent half a year painstakingly scraping together every possible penny, working long hours while postponing our future for one singular goal. And then it didn't happen.

That is the messiness of adoption and the terrifying nature of following God's will. God doesn't always get what God wants, at least in this life. And following God's will does not ensure a perfect and tranquil life. You can do everything right and still not have things work out the way you want. There will be times in this journey when you will question if this is God's will. You cannot define God's will by what is easy or successful. You can only be obedient, vulnerable, and full of love.

Nine Heartbreaks, Ten Cheers

Not knowing what else to do, we kept moving forward, putting our names on a list of prospective adoptive parents. We had followed God's will down this path, doors had closed, and what was left seemed like a long, narrow hallway with no exit. We grieved. We continued with our lives. We waited.

To go on this journey means putting yourself in a vulnerable place—financially, emotionally, spiritually. In our case, with domestic infant adoption, we submitted profiles of our family to moms for whom we met initial criteria. They would receive a book that we put together telling our family story, along with nine other books from nine other families all doing the same thing. The mom would choose her child's family from those ten options. This choice is a beautiful and empowering experience. But it also means that nine families will be told no, and their pursuit of a child will continue. After this happens to your family about a half-dozen times, you start to wonder if it's you. And then you start to wonder if you've misheard God and this isn't God's will for you after all.

In the middle of all our waiting and amid all the rejections, one of the "potentials" came from a mom who didn't know she was pregnant until abdominal pains sent her to the hospital. We were asked to submit our profile. We weren't chosen. Rejection number whatever. In the wake of that, Kelsie wrote this:

They give the mom ten families to choose from.

You grew silently. You didn't tell anyone you were there.
You didn't exist loudly.
You simply were, quiet and hidden.
You were born with surprise and confusion and chaos
instead of cheer and thrill and anticipation.

She made a quick choice, a safe choice for you,
a safe choice for her.
She didn't know you *were*, two days ago—
how can she *be* everything you need? how can she,
suddenly,
reorient her entire life because
you are?
She made a wise choice.
She made a loving choice.

The world was quiet when you were born.

She chose from ten families.

Nine of us ride this rollercoaster again and again.
For nine of us this is heartbreak number—
who knows? who keeps track anymore?

But maybe nine heartbreaks is worth
ten cheers,
in ten different states,
in ten different homes,
when we learned of your existence.
No one should be born uncelebrated.

I'm so happy you exist, little one.
I'm so happy you were born.
When I heard of it, I shouted for joy,
and so did the corners of the nation,
so did the hearts of many.

When I heard of it, I loved you instantly.

This is all we'll ever meet.
But it was a joy to know *you are.*

That is the story of adoption. It's a hard and messy road, and you shouldn't go down it without an understanding of what it will do to you, of how it will change you, of how difficult yet rewarding it will be. I'm a bit worried that I'm scaring you off the path, but what I want to do is share how much the prayers in this prayer book are needed.

There will be times when you don't know what to pray, and this book will guide you. Friends and family will ask what they can do, and the answer will be to pray prayers that look like the ones in this book. The beginnings of the journey are hard. But they're hard for the first parents too, whether the decision to place their child in the arms of another family is voluntary or involuntary, temporary or permanent. The weight we bear, the sacrifice we give, is all part of the process of redemption that adoption brings. It costs something to redeem something. Redeeming a life costs a life. *Maybe nine heartbreaks are worth ten cheers.*

Go until God Stops

We waited six months, during which we failed to match with a first family almost a dozen times. Then we got the phone call. *There's a baby that's been abandoned and referred to us. There's one other family ahead of you on the list. If they say "no," will you say "yes"?* This wasn't how we wanted it to be. We wanted to be chosen by a first mom. We wanted our child to know who their biological family was. This wasn't our plan at all. But again, how do you say no to a baby without a family just because their existence and their need doesn't fit your ideal?

We decided: If we said yes to the wrong thing, God could shut it down. God would be able to say no. We said yes and we waited. Five minutes later we were informed that the other family had chosen to adopt the baby. Devastation once again, but this time there was confidence that God was leading and directing our paths. It's difficult to say things like this when we see God working through tragedy and loss. Is God leading us into suffering simply for the sake of what's on the other side? Was it God's will that our adoption failed and we remained on this journey of waiting and wondering? I don't have a strict theological answer to that, but while I believe God creates beauty from ashes, I don't believe God makes the ashes. Kelsie and I had been through a lot of ashes, but they were becoming the remnants of a refining fire.

A month later, it happened again. The call came while my wife and I were driving to church for the midweek youth service, which I was leading. *There's a baby that's been abandoned. You're at the top of the list. It's fully your choice to say yes or no.* This time it was completely on us. If we said yes, would God be able to say no if it wasn't God's will? God had already proven to do so. We asked the agency if we could have thirty minutes to talk it over. We made our decision before we reached the church parking lot.

I walked into the church service and began by breaking the news to the couple dozen high schoolers who had showed up. I told them I was distracted, but I'd do my best to lead through the service. At that point, Kelsie was on the phone with the agency in one of the classrooms. We started in prayer, giving thanks for God's love and mercy, that God was putting an end to what seemed an interminable journey. During a break for small group discussion, Kelsie slipped back in the room and told me that she was working on our travel arrangements to leave the following day. I cannot tell you what message I preached or whether or not I was any good at preaching it. We were finally having some resolution.

Maybe twenty minutes later, in the middle of my message, Kelsie burst back into the room sobbing. There was a legal technicality specific to the state we lived in that prevented us from adopting the baby, something the agency only caught when reviewing our paperwork. It was a no once again.

In the New Testament, Paul is mounting a missionary journey eastward, but he isn't having success. He writes,

They went through the region of Phrygia and Galatia; they had been forbidden by the Holy Spirit to speak the word in Asia. When they came to Mysia, they tried to go into Bithynia, but the Spirit of Jesus did not allow them. . . . During the night Paul had a vision in which a Macedonian man was standing and pleading with him, "Cross over to Macedonia and help us!" After he had seen the vision, we immediately made efforts to set out for Macedonia, concluding that God had called us to preach the gospel to them. (Acts 16:6-10)

Paul didn't wait around. He didn't say wait for God to say "Go!" He went and listened for when God said "Stop." We knew we were called to adopt, so we took a similar approach. We planned to go unless God said stop. We knew God had given us this decision. We were going to say yes. If God wanted to stop it, God could. This time, God had. Yet, less than forty-eight hours later, we were on a plane—*finally*—to see our new daughter.

Resolution

The agency called us the next day. *You won't believe this, but there's another baby, and the mom is asking that we choose the family. It all works out this time. We've checked. No legal issues.* That was at midnight, and we left late afternoon the next day. We got on a plane, and I'd like to tell you there were no more problems, no more scares that this might not be, no more worries that our lives would be shattered once again. But I would be lying. Even so, we took that baby home with the blessing of her first mom, and I cannot imagine having any other daughter.

Our story has been a long journey down a broken path. Adoption and fostering often begin in tragedy. Whatever caused a child to not be raised in, or to be taken from, their first family—whether death, addiction, abuse, or lack of resources or readiness—meant the people involved had to make difficult decisions, perhaps in the midst of trauma. When you commit to being a foster or adoptive parent, you're stepping into that difficulty and trauma, which means you must step lightly.

The rosy beginning of the story for the adoptive family is a turbulent middle chapter—or ending—for the adopted or foster child and their biological family. And joining that story means engaging in the turbulence. The story of adoption isn't about us as parents but about the children we welcome into our families. I would go through the heartbreak again if it meant having the children I have. The road will not be easy, and this is only the beginning...but let me tell you that it's worth it.

Life Turns on a Dime

Throughout our adoption journey, we survived on prayer and the Christlike hospitality of friends and strangers. The number of people who opened their homes, their bank accounts, and their hearts to us was absolutely overwhelming. God works through God's people and their prayers. Early on, in my son's adoption, a coworker told Kelsie about asking for a sign from God in the form of a dime. Later that day, she opened a random drawer in a desk that had just been assigned to her, looking for a cable. The desk was empty . . . except for a lone dime.

The dimes kept piling up—more than enough to call it coincidence, found in the oddest of places. And then, at the end of the day we first met our son, we stumbled into a fast-food restaurant and found a dime lying right there on our seat. It was a reminder of God's faithfulness and provision. God had been there all along, answering prayers and drawing us closer.

If you're on an adoption or fostering journey, this prayer book is your survival kit. My hope is that it will bring a sense of community for you, wherever you are on the path and whatever your role is. Not every prayer will apply to your situation, but every prayer applies to thousands of people across the world. If you don't need to pray it for yourself, pray it as an intercessor for others. May these prayers be blessings for you on your journey, lights amid darkness, strong supports in a time of weakness, dimes in unlikely places. Beginning this journey isn't easy, but the reward—and the redemption—it brings are worth everything.

---

1. A Prayer as the Adoption Process Begins

To the God of Beginnings and Endings,
God who has loved and lost and loved and redeemed, God
    who has stepped into a human body and felt the pain of
    loving, of loving children, of loving children
who did not spring forth from the Creator's body
but were beloved by God nonetheless;
To the God of Creation and Community, the God who
    looked at one lonely human and said, "It is not good,"
the God who created family,
and parents, and children,
the God who is Father and Son
and the adoptive Father of countless more;

To the God who guards the hearts of those choosing now to
    risk themselves,
for "to love at all is to be vulnerable"—
To the God of the vulnerable,
to the God who made himself vulnerable with us,
To the hands of that very good and loving God, we entrust
    this often long and difficult process steeped in the
    broken reality of our broken world
in the trust and hope that you can redeem it, for you redeem
    all things,
Redeemer God.
Amen.

—*Kelsie Olds*

2. A Prayer for Parents Waiting-to-Be

O Holy God,
It is the time of waiting.
We are waiting,
Longing,
Hoping,
Praying,
Promising.
Promising a good life filled with love to this little one we can
    only imagine.
This little one who is not real until the phone rings.
This little one who may be growing even now, nurtured in a
    birth mother's womb.

Give us patience to wait.
Give us strength to keep hope.
Comfort us in the longing we hold deep inside.
Grow our hearts so that they might have endless room for
    this coming new life.
Remind us of the joy that led us down this path to begin
    with.
Let that spark a flame that continues to burn day and night,
    night and day,
Until the hour finally arrives and we hold our precious little
    one for the first time.
Amen.

—The Rev. Joey Heath-Mason

3. A Prayer when the Phone Rings for Placement

RING

This is it. No time for second-guessing.

RING

Give me presence of mind. Let me hear your voice, your
guidance, as I listen to the information. Remind me that if
it isn't a clear yes, it's a no.

RING

Speak loud, Lord. *Shout!* Help me hear the right voice over the static in my head and my heart and my stomach. Be with this child, Lord, right this very minute. Be with me too. My heart. Oh, my heart.

RING

You hold the future. You see the beginning and the end. Help. Now.

ANSWER

—*Marissa Joyce*

4. A Prayer for a Faithful Adoption

Good and gracious God, we thank you that you have adopted us into your family through the redemptive work of your Son.

We give you thanks for all the times you welcome us back when we, like the prodigal son, wander from you.

We thank you that you chose the humble Joseph as an example of love and nurture for your Son, whom he adopted as his own.

We give you thanks for bringing this family together, and we ask your blessings upon them as they provide love and support for one another.

Bless the home that they will share, and grant wisdom and understanding to all who will provide care.

Bless and strengthen their faith, and preserve them always by your grace.

We ask this through Jesus Christ our Lord, who lives and reigns with you and the Holy Spirit, one God, now and forever. Amen.

—*The Rev. Peter Preble*

—☙

5. A Prayer from an Adoptee's Perspective

Papa God, here I am. Do you remember me? Papa, my birth mom and dad can't take care of me right now. I don't know if they will be able to while I am growing up. It's so confusing for me, and I don't recognize the things and people around me. I ache inside. Papa, what will become of me? Is there anyone who will ever love me and take me home? I would like to know my own bed. I would like to be fed when I'm hungry and given something to drink when I'm thirsty. I want to be held, Papa, with love that won't stop.

Papa? Have you chosen someone for me? I see a face that smiles but with tears in those eyes. Strong arms scoop me up and hold me so gently, a happy tear even plops on my face. There are more faces, all with happy smiles and some with more tears. I am smothered in gentle kisses; I am held, and I am loved.

Later, Papa, they tell me about Jesus and that I have never been without you, that you will never ever leave me. It was because of you, Papa, that they found me. Because of your love they fell in love with me. You remember me, Papa. Because of your love, I have a family. I have a home. Amen.

—*Jennifer Lawrence*

6. A Prayer for beyond Our Imagination

I give thanks for your hands and feet, your nose and ears, and the way your hair blows in the breeze . . . though they look different than mine they are yours, perfectly and wonderfully made.

I give thanks for your laugh . . . the very sound of it reverberates through our family home and shows the joy that bubbles up from within you.

I give thanks for your hand in mine . . . we are journeying on this adventure together, through the hard times as well as the delightful ones.

I give thanks for your brain . . . the way you experience the world helps to open my eyes to the wonder of it all.

I give thanks for the ways we overcome obstacles together . . . for the other side is made that much sweeter because we are together.

Generous God, you have given us this family in a way we never could have imagined. Though we came together through heartache and amid suffering, we have pledged ourselves to one another just as we are. Be ever nearer to us as we struggle to adjust to one another. Be revealed to us in the ways we learn to love and trust each other. And through all of our shared experiences, we look to you as our guide for eternal love and companionship. Help us keep our focus on lifting up one another as you have united us as a family. We give thanks to you for helping us find each other through the hardest of times. We speak these prayers in thanks for our savior, Jesus Christ. Amen.

—The Rev. Paige Alvarez Hanks

7. A Prayer for the First Night of Placement

Yesterday, I was someone different. Today, I am a parent. Tomorrow is yet unknown. In all of it, I am yours, God.

Lord, grant me the grace I need to know that I am a new part of this child's story, and there is more to them than I see or understand.

Lord, help this child to feel safe here, to rest easy, to gather in sleep what they need to survive and thrive another day. Though it is scary for them, guide their heart towards trust. Help them to experience moments of true joy, and let those moments multiply in our time together that is to come, however long or short that may be.

Like manna, you do not give grace in a lifetime supply. You continually provide it one day at a time in perfect portions. Help me trust that you have given me and my child exactly what we need to flourish, just for tonight. Tomorrow is another day.

Thanks be to God.

—Laura Knobel

8. A Prayer at the Realization of the Need to Adopt

Lord,
We commit unto you this adoption journey, not knowing where it will go, fully trusting in you for every twist and turn along the path. Give us clarity of mind and purity of heart as we follow where you lead.

We pray for the birth family and the circumstances that have led to this adoption. We recognize that a family breaking apart was not your plan, and we are humbled to be a part of the messy redemption that adoption offers.

Search our hearts, O God, and see if there is any impure or selfish motivation within us.

Divest us of our pride and selfishness.

Drive from us all sense of judgmentalism and saviorism and superiority.

Give us patience in the times of waiting, when it seems like the journey will never end.

Grant us peace in the times of turbulence, when the journey seems different than we ever thought it would be.

Provide us with a strong support system to see us through from beginning to end.

Father, this is bigger than us. We cannot do it alone. Our lives will be forever altered by this decision, no matter the outcome. We step forward on faith and reliance on your calling, and we commit all of this to you.

Amen.

—*The Rev. Josh Olds*

9. A Prayer for International Adoptions

Creator God,
From all places and nations, you have called us to be your people. In our own discord and disunity, we falter. Call us to be your people once more. Bless this adoption across country borders and the process that it has inspired. Help us to love through it and find ourselves blessed by it. Keep us together as you call us to be together. This we ask in the name of your son. Amen.

—*The Rev. Robert W. Lee*

10. A Prayer for Foster Care and Adoptive Social Workers

God of wisdom and understanding, we lift foster care and adoptive social workers up in prayer. This is a job that carries the weight of being responsible for the lives of children, often in less than ideal conditions—too many cases, too many budget constraints, too many angry birth parents or angry foster or adoptive parents, too little control over decisions that affect the lives of the children in their care.

May these workers find their way through the complex problems they face each day, may they receive the support they need to do their job well, and, in the midst of all of it, may they keep the child's best interest close to their heart. May they experience the joy of helping a birth family be reunited or, when that is not possible, the joy of helping a child find a new forever home. And may they see you in the faces of the children and birth parents and foster and adoptive parents with whom they work. Amen.

—The Rev. Cindy Cushman

—ᏙᏗ

11. A Prayer for an Adoption Referral

Eternal God, all of our lives are in your hands. As I prayerfully consider adopting the child referred this day, help me listen not to my fears and anxieties but to your still, small voice as you guide the right decision not only for me but also for your child, who is fearfully and wonderfully made. Grant clear discernment and peace with the decision so I may trust that the choice is right for all concerned. This I ask in the name of Jesus Christ, who lives now and forever with you and the Holy Spirit. Amen.

—The Rt. Rev. Frank Logue

—ᏙᏗ

12. A Prayer of Commitment on Referral Day

Most gracious and loving God, every person is created in your image and likeness, yet with joy, wonder, and delight I learn of one particular child, referred for adoption. After prayerful discernment, I commit to the placement with gratitude, and I ask that you bless the birth parents, watch over this child, and guide this process. Walk with us through every remaining step, making straight the path that will bring us together. We ask all of this through Jesus Christ, our Savior. Amen.

—*The Rt. Rev. Frank Logue*

13. A Prayer for Deciding when to Say Yes to a Placement

God, you who know this child and every child, guide me.

Help me to decide if our household could be a place for healing for this child.

Help me to ask the most helpful questions, to think through the logistics of what this child needs.

May your Holy Spirit's wisdom be clear, and may the still, small voice of your guidance be strong.

And even as I make a decision, may I continue to pray for this child and all that they are experiencing. Amen.

—The Rev. Heidi Bolt

—̵ᴄ͡ᴐ

14. *A Blessing for Adoptive Parents*

May you be blessed with the courage to face your fears, anxieties, and doubts . . . because God is there amid the fray.

May you be blessed with the comfort of knowing you aren't alone, despite your own reasons to feel incredibly alone.

May you be blessed with laughter in your house and toys in your walkway—for you will see the grace of having enough.

May you be blessed with comfort in knowing your children were complete before you and will be complete after you have raised them.

May you come to know the fullness of words like *family*, *ballet*, *Star Wars*, and *Christmas mornings*.

May you be blessed with recitals, proms, graduations, weddings, and more . . .

And when it is all said and done, may you have the vision to look back and see that you waltz in, both blissfully unaware

and with eyes wide open to the most important thing that
has ever happened to you.

—The Rev. Robert W. Lee

15. A Prayer for Uncertainty

Lord, I am impatient. Waiting feels impossible! This process
is stressful, anxious, vulnerable, and frustrating at times. It
is also hopeful, expectant, and exciting.

God, I pray that you will reveal to me what is needed
and guide me to the right child or children who need me.
I have to make so many hard decisions; the list of names
is long and the challenges the children face are many. It is
sad and scary to have to say no, and I worry about those we
are leaving in your hands because we cannot welcome them
into our home. Please watch over them and call the right
family to them.

In all of this waiting I strive to embrace the lesson you
are teaching me—that I must know how to hold joy and
grief simultaneously if I am to love a hurting child. Please,
God, help me use this waiting time to look inward and
become the best person I can be in anticipation of the challenges to come. Let me learn to put aside my "stuff" so that
I may be more prepared to take on another's.

Finally, let me count knowing you, O Lord, as more
valuable than any blessing you have asked me to wait for. In
your holy name I pray. Amen.

—Laura Knobel

16. A Prayer for Adoption Day

Eternal Parent,

We became your beloved child not in the water of a womb but in the waters of baptism. In that adoption, you called us "Beloved."

As I hold this child near my heart, they and I are bound not by biology but by the cords of everlasting love. Grant me, my Loving Parent, the grace to share with my child a love that transcends the limits of this sphere so that they may garner a glimpse of the Divine.

And, in that same grace, may we find strength in the hard times, hope in the despairing moments, forgiveness in disappointment, and love as the bedrock of our shared journey. Watch over us as we live this life together, and when our respective time here is accomplished, draw us to you, our Eternal Parent.

Thank you for calling me "Beloved." Thank you for allowing me the privilege of speaking those sacred words to my child.

Amen.

—The Rev. Rob Rollins

17. A Short Prayer before Meals

Offered every night at dinner

Dear God we hope you have a good day in heaven, we hope you have healthy food, thank you for our people. Amen. **All: Amen.**

—*Athena Lee (age 4)*

_C3_

18. A Prayer for Respite Weekends and Nights

Dear God, in adoption and foster care we are reminded that grace is both cumbersome and liberating. We are excited and overwhelmed at all the decisions, prospects, and adventures to be had. Help us find rest in your love for the sake of our kids and ourselves. Help us claim and reclaim sabbath rest. Help us find our respite in you. Keep us close and keep us sane. Amen.

—*The Rev. Robert W. Lee*

_C3_

19. A Prayer for the Person This Child Will Become

Lord of Love and Hope, may this child flourish and grow into the person you have created and called him to be. May he be filled with compassion for others and hope for the world. When he is tempted to sink into despair, may the hope of this home and your great love lift him up. When he is afraid, may the safety of your arms calm his fears. May he one day feel true joy in the depths of his spirit and rejoice that he is your child, with just the right genes, experiences, and faith to make the world a better place as only he is able to do. This I pray in the name of Jesus, our Savior. Amen.

—*The Rev. Amanda Hines*

20. A Prayer for a White Parent Fostering or Adopting a Black Child

O God, I prepare to bring this child into my heart and home and family, I know there is so much I don't know and can never know about what it means to be Black in America.

As such, I pray that you help me

examine and challenge the racism that is inside me,
be aware of the privilege that comes from my skin color that my child does not share,

change my life in whatever way is needed so that I do not
raise this child in white-only spaces,
celebrate my child's Black identity and culture and incorporate that into our family culture,
seek out Black aunties and uncles who can give this child
what I cannot—a better understanding of their identity as
a Black person,
surround this child with such love and care that when they
look in the mirror, they see the face of God.

In Jesus' name. Amen.

—*The Rev. Cindy Cushman*

21. A Prayer for the Mental Health of an Adoptive Child

Father-Mother-God,

We lift up a prayer affirming your impartial and unconditional love for all whom you have created. We affirm that
you created all—every individual identity that has ever been
born or will ever be. Every man, woman, and child is created
in your image and likeness, pure and perfect. No matter
one's human history, each one is precious and prioritized in
your family of humankind.

We pray that your all-knowing grace will be especially
present with adoptive parents who are walking forward each

day as diligent, committed, loving parents, sometimes navigating the terrain of the unknown.

We pray that parents who have created loving and embracing families through the process of adoption rather than birth will feel your assurance, guidance, and wisdom when traces of unknown history, difficult influences, illness, or abandonment surface in their innocent beloved children.

We especially pray that any signs of mental illness in their adoptive children will be faced with gentle awareness and knowledge that support is available—not identified as conditions of stigma or shame or confusion as sometimes suggested by an uneducated surrounding culture.

We pray that adoptive parents feel bolstered with the helpful awareness that mental health challenges have a brain-based origin, are not in any way connected to evil, and can be treated and brought into balance with professional assistance.

We pray for patience, clarity, strength, and support for adoptive parents facing these symptoms in their children, and for the fortitude to take one step at a time toward treatment and healing. We pray that they find communities of support and understanding.

This prayer is also for the children themselves. In cases where mental illness is part of the path of love to be lived, may God's ever-present love, healing power, grace, and unfailing presence be tangible in the lives of these families, and may the one Father-Mother-Love be a guiding light felt by all.

—Sue B.

22. A Prayer for Birth Parents

Gracious God who knows and loves us deeply,
We come lifting birth parents up to you.
We do not know all the circumstances that came together to
    create this new life.
We do not know the moments of angst and grief that they
    have gone through.
We do not know the struggle that led them to their decision.
We believe that love, in its many forms, has guided this
    decision.
We believe that your grace surrounds each one of these
    parents.
We believe that all hurts can be healed.
Bless these parents and honor all their reasons for making
    this difficult decision.
Hold them in your loving arms.
Let your face shine upon them and give them peace.
And may the love shared with their child be a blessing to
    them as well.
Amen.

—The Rev. Joey Heath-Mason

23. A Prayer for One's Birth Parents in Troubled Situations

God, I am angry that they made bad choices. I am angry that they cannot take care of me. I am sad that they hurt me. But I still want them to have a good life. Take care of them, God. Help them make better choices. Even if I never see them again, help them to become the people I always needed them to be. Thank you, Jesus. Amen.

—*The Rev. Amanda Hines, Katie (age 13),*
Xavier (age 11), and William (age 10)

—☙

24. A Prayer for Birth Mothers

Lord, father, mother of us all,
We wonder about our true origin—
Where we really came from
Why we are here.
Paul tells us that "when the fullness of time had come,
God sent his Son so we might receive adoption as children."
We ponder the greatness of so many who were adopted:
Moses, Esther, Leonardo da Vinci, James Baldwin,
Nelson Mandela, Superman, and Harry Potter—
All orphans.
Jesus, speaking to them and all of us
Hours before his death, promised us all:
"I will not leave you orphaned."
Thank you for birth mothers who don't abandon their
   children

So much as they relinquish a child for life.
Jesus relinquished his comfort and ease
Only to be abandoned by those closest to him.
No wonder he empowers us to cry,
"Abba, Father!"
Assured it is the Spirit himself bearing witness with our spirit
That we are children of God.
Thank you for welcoming us into a family
Not of flesh and blood
But of the Spirit, of love, of God. Amen.

—The Rev. Dr. James C. Howell

25. A Second Prayer for Birth Parents

Father God, who knew the loss of watching other people
    raise his child, you have lived the experience of a birth
    parent,
from knowing that people might call your child names,
or poke fun at his parentage,
through the pain of living without being able to protect him
    from everything, the pain of knowing the people who
    raised him would sometimes fail him, the aching and
    longing of bringing him into existence
and then letting him live a life on earth outside of you.
You knew it intimately;
you understood it wholly.
From his birth to his death, you knew it and understood.
Father God, who might have been called by other names,

who might have gone by Birth Father,
by Biological Father,
by First Father of Jesus himself:
bring comfort and healing to the parent who wears the same
    title that you have.
When no one else around them can understand what they
    are going through, you can, and you have.
When their story is secret and they have no one with whom
    to share it,
you hear, and You understand.
When their story is an all-too-public shame and an all-too-
    present reminder,
you are not their Judge but their Protector.
In a story centered on the new child and what is best for
    them,
they are your child,
And they were Your child first,
before this child ever began.
That you love them so fiercely,
that Your love for them never changes,
that you want what is best for them.
Father God, who turns all heartache and sadness and anguish
    to eventual redemption, the path is long and we do not
    see the end of it from where we stand,
but we trust in your guidance as we take the next step,
and we fall back on your everlasting love.
For the peace that passes all understanding we pray. Amen.

                                          —*Kelsie Olds*

26. A Prayer for Questions about the Past and Family History

God of our past, present, and future,

Be with all of those whose past includes trauma of any kind. Especially be with this dear child in my care right now who is struggling to learn about their past, make sense of their past, and incorporate their past into the person they are and will become.

Be with me as I seek to respond honestly and lovingly to questions for which I may not have an answer or for which the answers might be painful. Help me to find words that are truthful that will also calm fears and provide comfort.

When the answers to questions are painful or confusing, or there simply are not adequate answers, may this beloved child find peace in you. Amen.

—*The Rev. Cindy Cushman*

Part 2

The Anything but Ordinary

Kimberly L. Carter

"All of us are in the gutter, some of us are just looking at the stars." —Oscar Wilde

The thing that influenced me to find my biological family was the feeling of being a tree without roots. I was abandoned at birth in the hospital where I was born and placed into foster care until I was adopted at the age of two into a permanent home. From the time I was adopted until I was thirty years old, I was plagued with questions about my identity and family of origin. My adoptive parents, who are now both deceased, encouraged me to seek the answers to my questions when I was ready to do so. When I was thirty years old, I felt like I was prepared to find the answers to my questions about identity, so I researched and found my family of origin, reached out to them, and have been in communication with them since that time. As you can imagine, the journey of reconnecting to my biological family has been both joy-filled and complicated. However, I do not regret this journey and have felt a sense of wholeness and connectedness that I had not previously felt.

In the past, I have often found it difficult to express the issues around adoption because the response from others is usually centered on being thankful that someone decided to take me, as the adoptee, into their home. While this sentiment is not entirely incorrect, it does not leave room for the questions and concerns that can arise with being severed from a birth family and placed into a family of different origins. Further, this response is steeped in a privileged view since often the person expressing this sentiment was not adopted, so they have a direct connection to their families of origin, knows important medical information, and was most likely raised around their biological family. I have found that if someone was severed from their birth family in any way, they usually have more empathy for the concerns expressed by an adoptee. Adoption can be a complicated topic for everyone involved, including the adoptees. While there are no easy answers or remedies to the difficult nature and questions involved with adoption, we should all be allowed to grapple with these questions and concerns. However, we may never arrive at a complete answer.

Being an adoptee can be challenging, especially in our socially connected world. As an adoptee, I find myself marginalized as someone whose experiences differ from the majority—precisely, as someone who did not grow up with the legal right to personal information such as my original birth certificate, the names of my biological parents, or any identifying biological details. For an adoptee, the exploration of and reconnection to the family line is often layered with extra complexities since the connection to the family of origin is usually severed at an early age, sometimes at birth. In our connected modern world, we can use Google to access answers to complicated questions, but some adoptees cannot get answers to basic questions like their birth parents' names, their medical information, and other vital pieces of information that most others can easily access.

Technology also allows many people access to DNA and genetic testing and other breakthroughs, so we can trace the origins of our family's roots back hundreds of generations in some cases. But this access is denied for some adopted people who may not have a connection to their birth family's information. Knowing one's identity and origin story is a fundamental human right that most people take for granted because they have instant access to this information. The reality of this disconnection to identity may lead to an existential crisis of identity and requires patience and empathy rather than judgment and quick answers. Having questions about identity does not take away the blessing of being adopted and welcomed into a loving home. These questions are an essential part of the adoption journey.

As Christians, we are all adopted into God's family, but as humans existing in a specific time and place, with ties to a particular family of origin, concerns and issues around the topic of adoption can be more nuanced. God invites us to grapple with these questions and thoughts without shame or fear as we wrestle through the meaning of our own existence, humanity, and life's journey. Facing challenging issues such as adoption, relinquishment, and questions about identity does not take away from our ability to simultaneously be thankful for God's grace, care, and blessings. Dealing with these difficult matters exposes our humanity and makes room for honesty in the midst of gratitude.

27. A Prayer for a Sibling Adoption

God whose name is Mother and Father and whose family extends through heaven and earth, thank you for the children with whom you have blessed me. You formed them and loved them long before I knew them, and my greatest desire is to care for them in your image.

Though they arrive together and from a similar place, let me not forget that they are each their own person. Though it will be difficult work, guide my parenting decisions to support their unique needs, that they may heal and grow in the ways they need most.

Please, Lord, help these siblings to find comfort in one another and to see one another as equals. Let them gather and feel security when it is needed, but grant them the insight to know when space and time are needed, too. Help them to grow in relationship while they develop as individuals and to respect one another along the journey that is to come.

Let me not lose sight of them and let them not lose sight of each other, as we all fix our eyes on you. In your holy name. Amen.

—*Laura Knobel*

28. A Blessing for Merging Families

God, whom did you knit in our mothers' wombs? Oh, was it all of us? Then help us to drop the pretenses of a biology that skews perceptions and hearts and kinship and leads to strangers not acting in love but in selfish curiosity. Make your creative biology our biology. Make your gracious heart our hearts. Make your unconditional kinship with Father, Son, and Holy Spirit our kinship. Make your unquenchable love our love. We beseech thee in the name of our Lord and Savior, your Son, Jesus the Christ. Amen.

—*The Rev. Will Hasley*

29. A Prayer from an Adoptive Grandmother

Dear Lord,
Please bless this family with everlasting faith that you will guide them in your glorious direction and that they will hear your comforting voice through the Holy Spirit. Cover them as they wait in joyful celebration of becoming a family, as one, under your making. Light their paths along their journey in becoming a forever family so that their walks through the valleys may be illuminated like the summits of the mountains! All glory to you, O Lord. Amen.

—*Kathleen Sansoucy*

30. A Prayer for Foster/Adoptive Parents of Children with Disabilities

Dear God,

Please help me to see and recognize this child for who they truly are. Help me to put aside my own agendas, fears, and desires, and allow me to see this child as you see them. Give me the wisdom to discern how you are calling me to best support this child at this time. Give me the wisdom and insight to seek out the help and support we need from skillful clinicians, teachers, and other professionals who can help this child grow in health, wellness, and strength. Give me the courage to accept this child's limitations and the forbearance to tolerate daily frustrations as well as bigger disappointments. Pierce me with your love and peace every day. Give me patience and joy in parenting this unique and wonderful person. Help me to recognize the gifts in this situation, knowing that this child is your child—a child of God, a child of pure love. Please bless our family as we continue to grow in your steadfast love, and shine your light upon us always. We pray these things in your holy name. Amen.

—*Kate Rademacher*

31. A Prayer for Celebrating a Baptism

Eternal God, on this baptismal day we pray that the waters that began when you swept across the darkness and brought forth light might be the same waters that lay claim to a hope we have for this child. Make clear your work imagined in us, through us, and by us. Help us to claim this child as our own through baptism as well, knowing they did not come from us but are part of us now and forever. Help us to seek out the claiming sense of grace and abundance this day and forever. This we ask in the name of the one who was baptized for us and like us, your son our Savior Jesus Christ. Amen.

—*The Rev. Robert W. Lee*

32. A Prayer for a First Christmas Together

God, who makes families from annunciations,
    we give you praise on this first Christmas together,
for bright eyes, twinkle lights, and the smell of sugar cookies.
We thank you for the memories you make beside us in the
    wait,
for stretching hearts open to a promise bigger than ourselves.

God, who makes families against all odds,
    you are not stopped by governors or kings;
    you make room for those in need.

We give you praise for creative innkeepers and steadfast
    donkeys,
for parents of flesh, parents of faith, and parents who are a
    bit of both,
        choosing trust over fear in the dark.

    God, who makes families from angel-song,
    we praise you for remembering shepherds in fields
    and for good news flung wide to all creation.
    We remember those alone this season,
    and open wide our door of welcome.

God, who makes families through the gift of love,
    we thank you for holding this world in your hands,
    not like a ball one might toss and drop
    but in the flesh of an infant Savior.
We thank you for holding us in your hands this Christmas.
Amen.

                            —*The Rev. Dr. Jerusha Neal*

33. A Prayer for Godparents of Adoptive Children

Almighty God:
You are a God of covenant. You are a God of kept promises.

We are a people of limited understanding.
Sometimes we believe our prayers are unanswered, and we
    forget to cast our gaze into a future we cannot imagine.

Forgive our lack of imagination.

You are a God of covenant. You are a God of kept promises.

When Abram and Sarai prayed for a child, you blessed them
    with descendants who would number more than the
    stars.
Sarai laughed. Isaac was born—the child of her laughter.
But before Isaac was born, Ishmael was conceived.
Ishmael, a child of promise. A child of the covenant.
Generation upon generation.
This is how you are faithful, Loving God.
From generation to generation.

You are a God of covenant. You are a God of kept promises.

You heard the prayers of Hannah and offered her the gift of
    motherhood.
She kept her covenant and shared the care of her beloved
    son with Eli.
Through Ruth and Naomi, you modeled for us how families
    are made.
After Ruth delivered Obed, the midwives said: Look! A
    child has been born to Naomi.

You are a God of covenant. You are a God of kept promises.

Every child born will be the recipient of your promise. Every
    child is born of your covenant.
Mothering God, you gave us birth. You have shown us how
    to love as we desire to be loved.
Bless all who become loving guides along a child's way.

Creator God, you know the labors of genesis.
You birthed the universe and all that is in it.
You rested.

You, Nurturing God, know the challenges of parenting.
The exhaustion, the frustration, the pure, unbridled joy.
You, God of the Ages, know that it is not right for one to
    be alone.
You have given us to one another as partners, that we
    might share in the labors and struggles of parenting and
    provision.

Bless the families born from choice, forged in decision, and
nurtured through commitment.

Bless those serving as godparents. May they be pillars of
    strength and models of faith.
Bless them when faith makes room for doubt.
Bless them when challenges in the system arise.
Bless them when they have more questions than answers.
Bless them when they have no answers to a child's questions.
Bless them when it is hard. Bless them when it is effortless.
Bless all who have said yes to being part of a child's commu-
    nity of care.

You are a God of covenant. You are a God of kept promises.
Help us to be people of kept promises, too.

Amen.

—The Rev. Mandy McDow

34. A Prayer for a Child

Holy One,
Bless this child
That they might grow and know love always.
That they might see your grace in the parents
who have chosen to receive them as their own.
That they might live life to its fullest
with the blessing of family.
That they might see your face
in the faces of those who now surround them.
Love them. Protect them. Raise them up well.
And may they return that love out into the world.
Be blessed as you are indeed a blessing.
Amen.

—*The Rev. Joey Heath-Mason*

35. A Prayer for When I'm Angry

Dear God, I really love my family, but sometimes they can get on my nerves. Help me to stay calm when that happens. I can get on their nerves a lot, too. Help them to stay calm when I am aggravating. Family is a tough thing, and everyone needs to get through tough situations, so God please help us all. Amen.

—*Katie Hines (age 13)*

36. A Prayer for Teenage Years of an Adopted Child

Steadfast God,
God-who-does-not-change,
the God of the beginning and the end
who promises to be "the same yesterday, today, and forever":
In times of change and turmoil we find some comfort
in the steadiness of you
as a rock
we can stand upon, that will not be shaken, that will not
    fall.
No times are more turbulent than teenage years.
Everything changes, sometimes too quickly even to breathe.
But you are always near, with every breath.

Author God,
the God who knows the first and the last
of every story ever written,
and who promises good and perfect things:
Be near to the child inside of the teenager
and the adult inside of the teenager,
the story of childhood already written
and the story of adulthood yet being transcribed;
Be near in the repeated re-understanding
and re-experiencing
and re-living
of things that hurt, and things that confused, and things
    that were too big to hold when they were understood,
    and experienced, and lived
by a child.

And be near as they still hurt, and confuse, and are still too
big to hold.
Carry these burdens. Steady our feet.
O God, a shoulder to cry on and a foundation to live on, we
cry out to you:
Be near, be near.
Amen.

—*Kelsie Olds*

37. A Prayer for Teenagers in Care

Almighty God, open our hearts to support teenagers in
foster care.
May they experience a stable place where guidance can be
given.
A place of support where they can learn important skills that
will help them into adulthood.
May you guide them to supporters and mentors who will be
patient and kind.
Help them to find their identity in you and in this world
that will lead them to a successful future.
Teenage years are full of tests and trials as they figure out
who they are.
Teenagers in foster care need an extra level of protection,
Lord, as they navigate between their past, present, and
future.
Lead them into your path, Lord. Let them see and feel your
love.

Let them trust that they are loved when they are feeling
   rejected.
Give them the strength to know that they are beautiful children of God, full of love to give.
Place them into a loving and supportive family who will
   guide them as they develop into strong and stable adults.
May they know you and know that they are surrounded by
   your love and protection.
Let them be at peace with their current situation, and let
   them know that they are safe in your arms.
Lord, be their soft place to land when they are afraid and do
   not know where else to turn.
Lord and Savior, please lay your healing hands on their
   broken hearts and bodies.
Give them the strength to persevere during this time of
   uncertainty.
Lord, in your mercy, hear our prayer!

—*Michelle and Valerie Rogers*

38. A Prayer for the First Day of School

O God, how can my heart live outside my body in someone
who wasn't made in it?

Watch over my child, O Lord, and keep them safe today.
And please, too, remember me and my heart, which I now
realize needed more protection than I ever imagined.

For all parents during this milestone, we pray for peace.
Amen.

—*Stephanie Lee*

39. A Prayer for School

Today, I picture my child as a lily pad. One farthest from
shore, experiencing rougher waters but rooted to the earth
with a longer stalk than the others. They are vast. They ride
the waves with an air of permanence and unsinkability.
Things may weigh them down, but still they reach for the
sun. Earth-tethered, heaven-tuned.

In this way, I send my child out into the world but under
your keeping, God. When I cannot be with them, please
watch over them as they navigate their day and the challenges that may arise. Grant them a calm body and mind
to focus on their work. Help them believe in themselves
and know that we believe in them, too. Allow their heart
to shine as they interact with their peers, and may their
teachers see each part of them along with the whole and
respond in kind.

Please, God, let my child never forget that even when waters
are rough, they are bound to me and to you inextricably,
without qualification or expectation that they be anyone but
themselves. Let them grow each day but not lose sight of
home. Grant them peace in their heart to know that while

school is their world right now, it is not the whole world, and there is more goodness to come on earth and in heaven.

In your Son's name I pray. Amen.

—*Laura Knobel*

40. A Prayer for Sad Nights

God, tonight they couldn't sleep. Body writhing, twisted up in their blanket. Making some sounds I don't instinctively understand but am trying to learn. Mourning, crying, pain. Trusting is hard. Grief comes in waves. Pain is unpredictable. Your power is made perfect in weakness. In the darkness I dream of someday knowing their sounds, their breath, their heart, and their mind, if you will let it be so.
Until then, I will be here. Please God, be with me here while I am here with them.

—*Laura Knobel*

41. A Prayer for LGBTQ Persons

Queer God,
God of the margins,
the God who created the binary and the vast spectrums
    between,

the God of night and day
and of twilight, dusk, dawn, sunrise, sunset;
the God of black and white
and of red, pink, purple, blue, green, yellow, orange:
You are the God of all of your children. You are the Father
    of all of your children. You are the Creator of all of your
    children. And what you create is good.
You are the God of love
and we only know how to love because of how you have
    loved us.
Oh, how people have used your name in vain! How people
    have claimed the name of Jesus over their own sins!
They have lied about who you are.
They have used your name in defense
of othering, of hurting, of casting out, of killing.
When you showed us so clearly while you were on earth that
    you welcome the other in,
that your hands are to heal,
that your words invite in,
that you would die rather than kill.
Let the church rise up and embrace those it has rejected;
let the church fall down and ask forgiveness from those it
    has wounded.
God who makes all things new,
make a new way forward for your people;
give us the direction to include all of your people, loving
    and accepting them for who they are, exactly who they
    are.
You made them.
You made them good.
Amen.

—Kelsie Olds

42. A Prayer for a Child Aging Out of the Foster Care System

To the God of Gethsemane,
the God who stepped forth out of heaven and into a human
    body,
traveled through the ups and downs of a human life,
to culminate trembling in a garden and knowing that every
    person you loved left you;
to the God who knows the depths of loneliness,
to the God who acutely understands feeling forgotten,
to the God who cried out to his Father, "why have you
    forsaken me"—
O God acquainted with sorrows—
we have your promise that you came to tend to the broken-
    hearted on earth
and your assurance that you can take even a heart of stone
    and make it into flesh.
We know that after a lifetime of broken promises,
it sometimes feels safer to harden a heart for our own
    protection.
And we know that you understand the depths of these
    emotions, too—
that you have stood here yourself,
that you have felt time slipping away,
that you have felt the deepest betrayal
by someone—many someones—who should have been
    there for you.

Lamenting the injustice, we find you beside us, weeping real
  tears over a fallen world. Picking up the pieces, we find
  you beside us, carrying the burdens of a lonely soul. And
  even though we walk through the valley of the shadow
  of death,
we are not out of your sight,
nor out of your presence.
When no one else is there, God Who Is There,
thank you for being.
Amen.

—*Kelsie Olds*

43. A Prayer to Celebrate Licensing as a Foster Parent

Gracious God, in your fullness you gave us the gift of
parenthood, knowing you yourself were a parent to your
son, our Savior Jesus Christ. Grant that as I am licensed for
foster parenting, I might remember your call to love without
regard to the cost. Help me remember that you are present
and working in both my life and the life of any child who
comes under my care. Help me be you for them, incarnate
and working for good. In your holy name I offer this prayer.
Amen.

—*The Rev. Robert W. Lee*

44. A Prayer for Coming Home
with Your Adopted Child

Long ago a woman by the name of Hannah prayed for a child, and God heard her voice and saw her tears and it was granted to her.

We too have prayed for a child, and God has heard our prayer.

Long ago a woman by the name of Hannah looked into the eyes of her new child and exclaimed:

For this child I prayed, and the LORD has granted the desires of my heart. (1 Samuel 1:27)

We too look into the eyes of our gift of God and believe that this child is the one for whom we prayed. The one who has fulfilled the *desires of my heart.*

God, we ask that you bless us with the wisdom to appreciate this great gift of life.
God, we ask that you bless our hearts with the ability to fully express the love that we feel for this child.
God, we ask you to give us the strength to build a true and faithful home in which to raise this child.

Praised are you, God, who has kept us in life and helped us to reach this blessed moment.

Amen.

—Rabbi Michael Siegel

45. A Prayer for Questions about the Past

God,
There is so much we do not know.
So much that remains hidden.
Yet you know.
There is so much we do know.
So much we do not know how to best pass on.
Yet you know.

With adoption comes the loss of a beginning of a story, and whether good or bad that story rightfully belongs to a child who deserves to have it. Help us answer their questions honestly, lovingly, and appropriately.

Give us strength to exist in the tension of not knowing, of wanting to know, of being scared to know, or of knowing and being scared to share.

Teach us to tell their story to them in ways that are honest and safe, ways that help them understand their loss, heal from it, and build security and identity that stabilize their future.

In your loving name we pray.

Amen.

—*The Rev. Josh Olds*

_⟨ℰ⟩_

46. A Prayer for a Closed Adoption

Omniscient Creator,

Part of a story ends here, and it hurts. And while you know all things, we may never know them. We pray for the parents of this child who may never know anything more about them. We pray that it was the right decision for them to make.

In the future, this little one will have questions that we will not be able to adequately answer. They will be hard and important questions. Prepare us for how to respond. May this little one know their identity in you even if it feels like a piece of them is missing. May they never feel unloved or unwanted. Exist with them in the tension of the unknown and uncertain. Carry them through the valleys as they wrestle with not knowing.

Begin a new story here, even as we lament the passing of the old.
Amen.

—The Rev. Josh Olds

_⟨ℰ⟩_

47. A Prayer for a Church Supporting an Adoption

Holy God,

You have adopted us into your family. We gather here today as brothers and sisters to support our own as they seek to be the image of you and adopt a child into their family. It's a holy journey that cannot be done alone, and we commit to being there for them every step of the way. We commit to providing support in any way possible: we commit our time, our finances, our resources, our presence, and our prayers. We commit to being the family of God and reaching out to make new members of that family feel welcome and supported. May this church grow in faithfulness and commitment to you through this journey. In your name we pray all these things. Amen.

—The Rev. Josh Olds

48. A Community Prayer to Bless and Affirm an Adoptive/Foster Family

Please extend a hand of blessing as we pray.

O God of life, through your boundless creativity, you call us to embody your very nature, which is relationship, community, and family. Even from the cross—in the softening heartbeat of your child, Jesus—you called a new family into existence, saying, "Here is your parent; here is your child." We stand in those deep and holy footprints today as you call together this new family. Pour your abundance upon *these people and this child* who seek your blessing and the support of this church community. As they come together as parent(s) and child(ren), watch over their going out and their coming in. Support them in their waking, in their sleeping, and whatever may come between. And finally, knit within them, and within all of us, your vision of justice, peace, and compassion.

In this moment and always, may they know that they are blessed, known, and affirmed in the name of God Creator, God Sanctifier, and God Redeemer.

Let the church now say, "Amen."
—*The Rev. Dr. Charles "Charlie" Dupree*

49. A Prayer of a Stepparent of Adopted Children

O God, the creator and lover of all souls,
the kids and I came into each other's lives when I married
    their dad.
Hopes were high for all of us,
desiring to be family.

I was naive to assume that they would be like me,

would somehow share my interests, my way of life,
even my personality traits.

Whatever issues they may have had from being put up for
   adoption by their birth mothers years before,
I figured we would talk about them.
Whatever issues they may have had from the death of their
   adoptive mom,
I figured I could encourage them to mourn, to get coun-
   seling as needed.
Whatever issues they may have had in their burgeoning
   adolescence,
I figured I could handle.
I had taught school and led youth groups, after all.

It didn't turn out that way.
They were created in your image,
not in mine.
They had a chemistry and DNA that was different from
   mine, different from their dad's.
They had reasons and resistance,
interests, skills, abilities and inabilities of their own.
Their otherness
often challenged, sometimes thwarted,
the visions I had
of what my family would be like.
Even as I challenged, sometimes thwarted theirs.

In time, we have grown.
All of us.
I have been able to seek their forgiveness and yours.
And I now can thank you.
Through them,

you have helped me learn to love those who are different
    from me.
To witness to them
the value of that love.
Through them,
you have expanded my vision of family,
and of the whole human family of God.

In the Name of the One who adopts us as his own,
Jesus the Christ.

—*The Rev. Lisa Fischbeck*

50. A Prayer for Those Waiting on an Adoption Match

God,
The way you make families is a mystery to us.
You are a mystery to us.
We do not know much for sure.
But we do believe this: you have asked us to wait.
You have asked us to wait for one or ones we cannot yet see.

We take on this waiting because we believe there are chil-
    dren in need of kinship with us.
We believe we can welcome one or ones whom we do not
    yet know.
We believe adoption is our gift of welcome that the world
    needs from us.

So here we sit. Days, weeks, months may pass. No news.
We wait.

We wait with expectations in our hearts.
We wait wondering—
When will we meet?
Where will we meet?
How will our story intersect with this face we cannot see?

God, we wish you could give us a magic eight ball that
would give us the answers we crave.
We grow weary in the unknowns of this waiting.
We grow weary in worrying about all the what ifs to come.
We grow weary in the dwelling on the disappointing possi-
bilities of what might happen.

We wait.

Teach us to live in the present as much as our heads are
already in the future.
Teach us to trust in roads we do not yet see ahead.
Teach us to love the unanswered questions as mentors for
what will come next.
Teach us that you are good.

Mysterious one, may we be renewed in the waiting, transformed in the waiting, encouraged in the waiting. We
cannot wait alone. Wait with us.

Amen.

—The Rev. Elizabeth Hagan

51. A Prayer for Entering a New Adoptive/Foster Placement

O God, whose Redemption sings "You are wanted!"
O Christ, who brought the children near,
O Spirit, who pours love into our hearts,

We give you thanks for adoptive parents
who make every child feel wanted.
We give thanks for the dearness of every child.
Bless, O God, parents who open their hearts
and bring children home.

We pray for children entering a new home.
Help them feel new love.
Give new parents your own steadfast love
and bring them friends to share their joy.

Now, may the God who has adopted us all
as your daughters and sons
give us hearts to receive every child,
that as we do we will receive the Christ who waits for us in them. Amen.

—The Rev. Dr. H. Stephen Shoemaker

52. A Prayer for Court Dates

I solemnly swear that the evidence I shall give will be the truth, the whole truth, and nothing but the truth.

Let it please the court to know that this child is legal property of the Most High God. De facto property of heaven, sealed and safe within the covenant love of our Advocate.

May your honor hear the spaces between the facts presented. The sleepless nights, the dutifully charted medicines, the tear-soaked pillows, the graham-cracker-scented giggles. Let the record state that this child has a life, a future, a story outside of trauma, medical records, drug-screening results.

This counsel would like to request a recess, time carved out from the back and forth of affidavits to allow this image bearer of God to inhabit a true childhood, free from fears of a new home, a new school, a new family. Sun-dappled afternoons and fingers sticky from ice cream.

This Amicus brief submitted as evidence holds that this human life is sacred. Impossibly loved by multiple mothers. Every thought perceived from afar, every tear collected in a bottle.

The Almighty Judge holds in contempt the brokenness of the world that has truncated the story of this dear one, reduced their sacred story to a paper trail of broken homes and broken hearts.

So help me God.

—Marissa Joyce

53. A Blessing for an Unknown Timeline

Beloveds, a blessing as you wait:

From the very beginning of this journey, you have known that your timeline was somehow different from the usual "family creation story" peddled by made-for-TV movies, social media feeds, and thirty-second commercial plugs.

And so . . .

In a world where solutions are presented at the end of thirty-minute scripted programs,

May you feel an invitation to sit with the divine presence in this sacred but unknown timeline.

May you know that your waiting is not wasted, and that even now—in this very moment—your longings are seen and known. Indeed, you are seen and known.

In a world where most people live with the illusion that somehow through "to-do" lists and calendars the clock can be tamed, manipulated,

May you know that you are unique because you are awake to the divine mystery that all of us dwell in a "now and yet not yet" reality of life.

May you feel the presence of God as you wait for the "not yet" longings of your heart and family.

In a world where efficiency and rushing are idols,

You are awake to the sacredness of each moment. You know that none of us are guaranteed even the next moment.

And so . . .

May you find the ordinary moments extraordinary.

May the time of waiting be filled with the sacred mundane.

May small gifts of time, like a shared laugh or a story read, become themselves a sanctuary of holy presence.

May you see each moment before the final signatures and court decisions as a gift.

For you during this time have given the greatest gift—the one thing we can never control or get back . . . time. Your attention is the most expensive thing you will ever offer another.

And so . . .

May your present be filled with the presence of God, and may you feel that today, just as things are in this liminal space, everything is on time. Amen.

—*The Rev. Sarah Heath*

54. *A Prayer for Difficult Days as a Foster Parent*

God, I need you. I need you because it feels like I have
nothing left to give. Troubling behavior continues, inter-
ventions don't show promise, the grief and the anger and the
fear and the trauma are too much. For all of us.

God, I need you. I need any reserve of strength that can be
found to keep taking it one day at a time. I need any new
insight or wisdom about what might help this child feel safe
and secure and loved. I need any reminders that the care and
attention and boundaries that we are providing today will
have benefits far into the future.

God, I need you. I need you because this work is so hard.
And so necessary. And this child needs people to show up
when it's hard. And to keep showing up over and over again
until they know that they are not alone.

God, I need you. Amen.

—The Rev. Heidi Bolt

55. A Prayer for the Adoptee's Journey

Dear Heavenly Parent:

Please help me to be at peace with my life as I walk the path set before me.

Please give me supportive and understanding parents, siblings, and friends who are willing to learn how to comfort me in the complexities of my existence and are willing to help me construct a shield from the rain of my tears that I may sometimes cry because of the complex nature of my life.

Please help them understand that my pain is not something I can always hide, and help them not to personalize my "whys."

And when I cannot find the words to express the Primal Wound that exists in my heart and soul, please help me see myself as whole, although I wrestle with being complete in ways that others may not.

When I harbor unspoken questions, doubts, or fears, give me the courage to express this to all who would be willing to hear with an empathetic ear, and allow me to emerge on the other side with an understanding that all who have walked the adoptee's journey before me and all who may come behind me most certainly can relate to some part of my questions and insecurities. Help me be certain that I am truly not alone, although at times it seems to me like I may be.

Most importantly, please show me your plans for me and the reflection of me that I need to see gazing back at me as I stare in the mirror to try to picture who may resemble me.

Please, God, help me walk the adoptee's journey graciously.

Amen.

—*Kimberly L. Carter*

56. A Prayer for Adoptive Parents

Loving God, who knit us together,
Thank you for the opportunity to share our love and life
    with this, your child.
Thank you for this new stage where we become parents to
    this precious soul.
Thank you for walking alongside us as we parent out of our
    love that comes from you.

Shepherding God who guides and guards us,
Help us to be patient with this child in our care.
Help us to love unconditionally, but guard our hearts from
    unintended hurt.
Help us to ask for help from those around us as we create a
    home of safety and love.

Eternal God who saves us all,
Give us courage to share your love, word, and goodness with
    our child.

Give us discipline to set aside the sabbath to worship you
   and to model worship for them.
Give us grace when we make mistakes, for Lord, we will.

Lastly, God, help us feel your presence in our home.
Wrap this special child in your arms and never let go.
We love you and thank you for your presence in our lives.
Amen.
                                          —*The Rev. Lauren Boyd*

57. A Prayer after Completing a Fostering/Adoptive License

Gracious Father,

We trust you today. We trust that paths have led us all to this
place and point. Of all the possible outcomes, you brought
us all here because you know best. We thank you for your
mercy and provision.

As you weave this time into the tapestry of our lives, may
you sew in threads of love where trauma has been present.
May you thread peace where anxiety once grew rampant.
May you loop in hope where time stopped, and grace where
all seemed menacing and cruel, unfulfilled and destitute.
All these things in this time and space. May this moment
be one that casts down past pain, to show us once again your
beautiful face, your plan revealed—one thread at a time. Amen.
                                          —*The Rev. Leo Morton*

—☙

58. A Prayer for Grace in Difficult Times

Dear God,
We are so often tempted to allow our hearts to be hardened. We feel anger, betrayal, mistrust, disbelief, hurt, fear, outrage, grief. Help us to remember that our emotions are part of your holy creation and therefore part of your gift to us. Allow us to honor and create space for all of our feelings. At the same time, Lord, please do not allow us to remain in a place of immobility or hardness of heart. Give us the grace to soften our minds and spirits so that we may remain open to all the ways the Holy Spirit is moving between us and within us. Protect us, Lord, we beseech you, in your eternal goodness. Amen.

—Kate Rademacher

—☙

59. A Prayer for When a Child Runs Away

God, keep her safe. I don't know what danger will come her way. I feel helpless. I cannot keep her safe. Please keep her safe for me and bring her back home. You know the depth of her pain. I have tried so hard, but I cannot do this alone. I need your help. She needs your help. Help her to trust me with her pain enough to come home. Help her to use her words instead of her feet. I am afraid for her. This family needs you. We need your strength. We need hope. We need peace in our souls. She especially needs you now. Keep her safe and bring her home, God. Amen.

—*The Rev. Amanda Hines*

Part 3

On Endings

Kate Rademacher

"Goodbyes always make my throat hurt." —Charlie Brown

The last time we saw our foster daughter was at an ice cream shop. Alyana's* adoptive parents and our family had agreed to meet in a neutral place for what we hoped would be a fun and relaxed visit. We all sat in the rocking chairs on the porch outside the store. Alyana, who was five years old at the time, told us about her bedroom at her new house. We expressed our excitement and support. I wiped the drips of chocolate off her chin before she ran off to play in the yard with my biological daughter, Lila.

That was the last time we saw her. In the weeks that followed, we learned from Alyana's adoptive family that this ice cream visit had serious emotional repercussions. Rather than serving as a time of integration and healing, the visit was emotionally confusing and disruptive. The adoptive family said they were sorry, but after consulting with Alyana's therapist, it had been decided that we could not plan any other visits.

That was three years ago. Alyana lives just a few miles from us. She goes to the same elementary school that Lila attended. But she is out of reach; we are not allowed to be a part of her life. We had to let her go.

In many ways, loving and letting go are the central challenges of parenting—and of life in general. We must love deeply and well during the time we have with one another, and then, when the time comes, we must let go. In the interim, we as parents—whether biological, step, foster, or adoptive—attempt to give our children the tools, resources, support, experiences, and insight they need to make their way in the world without us. This is often confusing and hard, but it is what we sign up to do.

It is often difficult because we have needs and desires, too. As much as we want to love unconditionally and with spiritually pure intentions, we also want the good stuff for ourselves. I didn't want to lose Alyana; when she left our home to transition to the family who would ultimately adopt her, we were assured multiple times that the plan was for us to stay in her life. The social workers knew how attached she was to us—and vice versa—and they wanted to do everything they could to facilitate a sustained connection. The adoptive family agreed. But then things changed. The situation was reassessed. As a result, we had to adjust our expectations and move on, despite our grief, disappointment, frustration, and heartache. Lila still talks about Alyana with deep longing and love.

And this longing makes sense. Because love—the love that God has for us and the love we have for one another—is about a desire for communion. For connection. We were created in love, and we are all part of God's unfolding, dynamic, beautiful, love-filled creation. The hard things we experience—the disappointment, the loss, the hurt, the pain—can feel antithetical to God's plan and purpose. But this may not always be the case. Change and growth are also part of God's creation. We cannot fully know where God is leading us, just as we cannot know what our children's futures hold. So we must let go in trust, while at the same time staying focused our most fundamental task of loving one another without allowing our own fears, insecurities, or despair to get in the way.

But what happens when separation or distance—or even death—*does* get in the way? How do we keep loving then? As people of faith, we are taught to love our neighbors as ourselves. The origin of the word neighbor is a term that means "one who lives near." It can be hard to love one's neighbor when you're not close to them, physically or emotionally. Fostering became an opportunity for our family to become close—on many different dimensions— to people we never would have encountered otherwise. That process was an honor, a challenge, and ultimately deeply enriching for all of us. But when we abruptly lost those connections, I experienced deep grief and anger, even though I knew no one was at fault.

Grief can be conceptualized as the gap between what we want and what we have, the world we wish for and the world as it is. The process of healing involves accepting those gaps and learning to find and encounter God in the broken, fragmented places, even as we long and pray for God to redeem and renew our broken world. In the meantime, even if we are not physically or emotionally close to one another, we can still focus on the spiritual work of loving our neighbors as ourselves.

One thing I've learned in connecting with many foster and adoptive parents over the years is that no two stories are the same; foster and adoptive families face a range of experiences, opportunities, and challenges, and every situation is unique. Yet every parent I have ever known (of all types) at some point has to go through a process of letting go. This can take many forms. The main thing is that whether we are separated from our child or children by distance, misunderstanding, interpersonal boundaries, disability, legal constraints, or even death, we can remain in communion with one another. In this process, we have the opportunity and invitation to love *and* to let go. This is the price and privilege of parenting. And ultimately, as parents, what is bigger and more important than that?

*Names changed to protect confidentiality.

---

60. A Prayer for When You Feel Abandoned

Are you there? God, I often feel abandoned like your son on the cross. Help me at least find solace in sharing in his suffering. Let me feel the grace of what is greater than myself with hope that it will lead me to you or to peace that is hard to understand. Help me love myself and others, I pray. Amen.

—*Pastor Jay Bakker*

61. A Prayer for a Mental Health Crisis

God, I didn't sign up for this—yet here we are. Keep my child in the knowledge of your love when all else fails. Keep them in your watch-care and give me sanity too. This is so hard. Yet your steadfast love endures forever, and it is enough. Give compassion to those who care for my child now—never leave them or forsake them. Keep them in the peace that passes all understanding. And if it's not too much to ask, some peace for me would be good too.

—The Rev. Robert W. Lee

62. A Prayer for the Frustrated Parent

Oh Lord, I am tired. Minute to minute, day to day, I work to be as compassionate as possible in the wake of the daily aftereffects of trauma, but it wears me down.

All I have ever wanted is to be a good parent to my child. I want them to know they are loved, valued, and capable. My actions don't always line up with this intent. My mistakes grate on my heart and replay in my mind.

I return to this request: for you to create in me a gentle heart, an unwavering spirit. Mold me in your image, one of forgiveness, flexibility, patience. Soothe my heart and mind when chaos reigns.

I know you are creating a clean heart in my child too,
God. But there is much work yet to be done. On hard days,
I struggle to see them as you see them—innocent, precious,
worthy. I ache to commune with their heart but find myself
only able to react to their behaviors. I feel hopeless.

Remind me, God, of how I see my child when I check on
them in their sleep: with immense pride and overwhelming,
heart-bursting, awestruck love—the way you look at both of
us, even at our worst moments.

On days like this when it is too difficult to go on, I lean
on your grace for respite. I cling to you. I breathe deeply and
know that you are as close as air. Amen.

—Laura Knobel

63. A Prayer for Saying Goodbye to a Foster Child

Dear God,

As we say goodbye to the child or children who have been in
our home, help us to know that we will always be connected
to one another through your love. Help us to know that our
love for each other is a gift, and that the many ripples this love
creates in the world will move outward in ways we cannot
anticipate and may never know. Help us remember—even
during times of loss and grief—that you are always with
us. Allow us to remember that any opportunity to love our
neighbor, including the children among us, is a chance to
be with you. Please give us the strength and courage to say

goodbye. Allow us to stay open-hearted, even when we are hurting, throughout this unfolding process.

—Kate Rademacher

―☙

64. A Prayer for the Marriage of Adoptive and Foster Parents

Dear God,

We are grateful for the holy sacrament of marriage as a place where two people show up in all of their diversity. Two people with different needs, perspectives, histories, desires, and ways of being with you and in the world. Please strengthen our marriage as we navigate this experience. Give us wisdom to take space when we need it, and give us grace to come back together in greater intimacy, openness, strength, and care for one another and for the children in our lives. Please help us weather the storms of this life, giving us courage to remain open-hearted and to listen to one another—including to the deepest longings in both of our hearts. We thank you and ask for your holy protection.

—Kate Rademacher

―☙

65. A Prayer for the Wedding Day of an Adopted Child

God, in your abundance you gave us so much—laughter, joy, and compassion. Today we share that with our child and their new spouse. May they cling to each other in times of turmoil, and may they celebrate each other in times of hope. May they subsist on love and be brought to completion in love. If children are their wish, may they find such grace that we have found in our time as their parents. May they find themselves more in love with you and with each other all the days of their lives. This we ask in the name of love embodied, Jesus Christ. Amen.

—*The Rev. Robert W. Lee*

66. A Prayer for a Blended Biological and Adoptive Family

Dear God,

As a new child or children enter our home, please bless and protect the children that are here now. Please give them strength and courage to open their hearts and lives with compassion and patience and love. Please protect all of your children so that they remain safe from all harm. Help us and all the adults in their lives to ensure that this is a safe place and that no harm befalls anyone in our care. We are all vulnerable in this situation, Lord, and we ask for your protection and guidance and wisdom. Help us to be shepherds, like you, so that none in our flock are lost or in danger, and so that all may return in love.

—*Kate Rademacher*

67. A Prayer for the Floor

God, who finds us where we are,
we find ourselves again beneath the kitchen table.
On the floor
is where so many things end up, God.
Toys dropped, crumbs scattered.
Shoes thrown, books smashed.
Jackets that will not zip, heaved across the room.
Juice flung in one mighty wave of frustration.
Because finding our words is tough.
And regulating our feelings is not as easy of a reach
as grabbing the nearest cup
and watching it smash
on the floor.
We kneel down, when the calm returns, and wipe it up
    together.
Side by side, in a ritual of putting things right.

May we see this space as holy ground, so that when we end
    up
on the floor
where the work of play happens,
Where the trains go round, where we crawl and build,

Where the grounding practices and the calming strategies
    bring us back
to ourselves, we can breathe and trust in your strength.
May we remember how trauma can snatch us from a happy
    moment to a past pain in an instant.
We sit, read, cuddle, and let our tears fall
Side by side, feeling safe enough to scream and
look in someone's eyes.

On the floor
is of course where we find you, too.
Overwhelmed with the patterns of parenting children
    through their trauma,
Knowing that screams and kicks and endless asks are simply
    a communication, a reach.
We crumple on the floor.
Seated cross legged, arms folded, heart unfolding,
and letting out one long breath
That you can hear.
And then one more. Breathing, to remember.
That there, on that bedrock for exhausted souls,
that firm floor that catches every stomp and splatter, is room
to breathe.
To let the tears of grief and gratitude fall,
to be still,
to be known and made whole
and stand again.
Amen.

                              —*The Rev. Dr. Erin Robinson Hall*

68. A Prayer for LGBTQ+ People in Foster Care

O Lord, hear our prayers this day.
There are children in foster care who need you.
All children need you and your love.
There is special care needed for LGBTQ+ persons in foster care.
O Lord, hear our prayer.
LGBTQ+ persons in foster care need to feel your presence.
They need an extra sense of love in their lives.
O Lord, hear our prayer.
This world can be cruel to them.
Help them find their support system even amid being displaced from their families.
Children are in foster care at no fault of their own.
Some parents are unable to care for them, and there are even sadder situations where LGBTQ+ persons are disowned and kicked out and end up in foster care.
They need to feel your love and peace.
Guide them into your loving care.
Show these special children that they are precious and worthy of love.
Guide them to find the support they will need in this life.
O Lord, hear our prayer.
Cover them with love when they feel rejected for being different.
Give them the strength to stay strong when they feel alone and secluded.
Give them the power to be themselves and know that they are loved.
Let them know that they are made in your image and that they are surrounded with your boundless love.

O Lord, hear our prayer.

—Michelle and Valerie Rogers

—⟡

69. A Prayer for High School Graduations

God in whom we have more beginnings than endings, we give thanks for the fullness of this moment brought to bear by the grace of your favor. You have enabled our child to reach new heights and new possibilities we never thought possible. Sometimes in our own doubt we have fallen short of being what our child needed—we pray for your forgiveness and theirs. But in this celebration, let us embrace the good that has been completed this day of graduation. May what is next bring you glory, and may what is behind show testimony to your great love through your Son, our Savior Jesus Christ. Amen.

—The Rev. Robert W. Lee

—⟡

70. A Prayer for a Child's Awareness of God's Love

Lord,
You have given me this child, but they were yours first.
You knew them before they were ever born.

You knew their thoughts, their desires, even their fears.

Before they breathed their first breath, you knit their body
    together.
Before they spoke their first word, you chose to love them.

For the rest of their life, I will love them unconditionally,
    unimaginably, and unreservedly.
But your love for them will forever remain the greatest.
Nobody will ever love them more faithfully than you.

Lord, I pray that they understand how much you love them.
I pray that they know you will never leave them.
And I pray that they know you view them as the apple of
    your eye.

Grant them the pleasure of following you.
Give them the honor of serving you in all they do.

This we ask in Jesus' name,
Amen.

—The Rev. Brandon Patterson

—͡໐

71. A Prayer of Thanksgiving

For those who wait for days that stretch into months,
O God, we pray for patience.

For those whose hearts have broken at the news of miscar-
ried dreams and unmatched hopes,
O God, we pray for comfort.

For those who wait for "yes," and for those who lie awake at
night wrestling with "no,"
O God, we pray for peace.

For those whose hearts nearly beat out of their chests at the
first sight of a single picture,
the spelling of a foreign name,
the name of a foreign land,
the phone call from a social worker,
O God, we rejoice and pray for fulfilled hopes.

For those who never dreamed they could afford it,
they could make it,
they could be called "Momma" or "Daddy";
For those whose dream is simply to love,
to share in the joys and frustrations of parenthood,
to watch with pride as a child learns and grows,
to be part of a life outside of their own,
O God, we give thanks and long for more to take hold of
their example of selfless love, grounded in your first love
for us.
Amen.

—The Rev. Dr. Chris Thomas

72. A Prayer for a Death in the Adoptive Child's Biological or Forever Family

God of Eternity,

Though the shadows of death have fallen over this your child, grant them the courage to face this reality in the fullness of your peace and presence. Help them to remember that though our lives are finite and fleeting, you are infinite and abiding. Be near to us now. Be near to all those who hurt because of death. May we know resurrection in our very bones. May we trust in your promises of life eternal and have the grace to live our lives in the presence of the Divine. This we pray in the name of the one who died for us so that we might live, Jesus Christ. Amen.

—The Rev. Robert W. Lee

73. A Blessing for a Foster Child No Longer in Your Care

Beloved Child,

May you laugh today because you have so much joy in your heart.

If today includes hard things, may you know that you have the skills and resources to handle the hard things of this day. If today is full of fun and learning and excitement, may you take it all in, knowing that you are worthy of all good things.

May you know that today and every day, I am thinking of you and praying for you and wishing you well. You will always have a place in my heart, and I thank God that I got the opportunity to know and love you, even if now it is from a distance.

May it be so. Amen.

—*The Rev. Heidi Bolt*

⟿

74. A Prayer for Those in Foster Care or Those Leaving Foster Care for Adoption

I know there are hands that have held you before

There were hands that held you tenderly, that supported
    your first breaths
Your introduction to this world

There were hands that cheered you on through firsts
Your first walk, first word, first joyous dance to a song you
    feel in your bones

There were hands that guided you through the dark
Through heartbreak, through grief, through anger that
    made you shake

There were hands that celebrated you as you became
As you grew, as you learned, as the seeds of you took root

Sometimes, I am jealous of these hands
These hands that experienced things already past

But so many hands shape the paths our lives take
And these are the hands that made you *you*

So I will send my gratitude to the lives who touched yours,
To the hands you carry with you

And I remind myself that my hands, too, have supported
  you
Have cheered for you, have guided you, have celebrated you
Now, and before, for as long as you've been here

For however long our hands find ways to fit inside each
  other,
know it is an honor to be the hands that hold you now.
  Amen.

—Frankie Boyko

75. A Prayer for Restoration

Dear God,
The world is so broken, and we ache for all of your children
who are hurting, who are lost, who feel unloved, who are
physically or emotionally unsafe, who are recovering from
trauma, and whose lives and futures are uncertain. Please
allow all of our suffering to be transformed in you and
through you. Please restore and remake this broken world

so that each child of this world is safe and whole and well. Please lift us up and give us your freedom, so that we may be in the world with resurrected lives and resurrected futures, and so that we may be ambassadors of your peace and grace on the road ahead.

We pray all of these things in your Holy Name. Amen.

—Kate Rademacher

76. A Blessing to Sum It All Up

God of all that has been, is currently, and will be in the future—may the road we walk always lead us home. Help us to realize that home is not defined by blood but by water of the Spirit. In that way, that water is always thicker than blood. May we be worthy of your calling to *adopt/foster* your beloved children, and may they feel the love we have found in you for all the days of their lives. This we ask because we need you now more than ever. Amen.

—The Rev. Robert W. Lee

About the Editor

The Reverend Robert Wright Lee IV (Rob) is an author, activist, commentator, and preacher. His work has been covered by MTV, *The View*, *New Yorker*, CNN, *New York Times*, NPR, and countless others. Rob is a native of Statesville, North Carolina, and graduate of Duke University Divinity School in Durham, North Carolina. He received his master's degree in theological studies in May 2017 with a focus in practical theology and homiletics.

Rob has written extensively for both secular and religious news outlets such as NPR's *Weekend Edition*, *All Things Considered*, and the *Washington Post*. He has regularly appeared on WUNC's *The State of Things*, CNN's *Tonight with Don Lemon* and other national news outlets. He has preached from notable churches such as the Historic Ebenezer Church in Atlanta, the American Cathedral in Paris, Rockefeller Memorial Chapel in Chicago, First Presbyterian Church in Birmingham, and Harvard's Memorial Church in Cambridge. He has lectured at the University of Chicago, Union Theological Seminary in the City of New York, the University of California at Davis, Arizona State University, and St. Michael's College in Vermont.

Rob is a collateral descendant of Confederate general Robert E. Lee and has been engaged as an activist in the field of racial reconciliation. In July 2020, he testified before the United States Congress on H.R. 970, a bill to remove a statue of his ancestor at the Antietam Battlefield in Maryland. In January 2021, Rev. Lee participated in the Inaugural Interfaith Prayer Service for President Joe Biden and has regularly written devotionals for Dr. Jill Biden. He also hosts the popular podcast *Beloved Journal.*

Rob was baptized and raised United Methodist at Broad Street United Methodist Church in his hometown, but he cherishes the wealth of traditions he's been afforded to journey with. He lives in Statesville, North Carolina, with his wife, Stephanie; daughters, Athena and Phoenix; and poodle, Frank. He's an avid autograph collector.